Primary School Teaching and Educational Psychology

THE EFFECTIVE TEACHER SERIES

Primary School Teaching and Educational Psychology

David Galloway and Anne Edwards

LONGMAN
London and New York

Longman Group Limited,
Longman House, Burnt Mill, Harlow,
Essex CM20 2JE, England
and Associated Companies throughout the world.

*Published in the United States of America
by Longman Inc., New York*

First published 1991

Second impression 1994

British Library Cataloguing in Publication Data
Galloway, David M. (David Malcolm) *1942–*
  Primary teaching and educational psychology. – (The effective
  teacher series)
  I. Title II. Edwards, Anne III. Series
  370.15
  ISBN 0-582-49716-7

Library of Congress Cataloging-in-Publication Data
Galloway, David, 1942–
    Primary school teaching and educational psychology / David
    Galloway and Anne Edwards.
    p.   cm. – (The effective teacher series)
    Includes bibliographical references and index.
    ISBN 0-582-49716-7 : £5.95
    1. Educational psychology. 2. Problem children–Education
(Elementary)–Great Britain. 3. Special education–Great Britain.
I. Edwards, Anne. II. Title. III. Series.
LB1051.G2184 1991
370.15–dc20   90-40686
                                                            CIP

Set in 10/12 point Times
Produced through Longman Malaysia, TCP

CONTENTS

EDITOR'S PREFACE

This new series was inspired by my book on the practice of teaching, (*Effective Teaching: a practical guide to improving your teaching*, Longman, 1982), written for trainee teachers wishing to improve their teaching skills as well as for in-service teachers, especially those engaged in the supervision of trainees. The books in this series have been written with the same readership in mind. However, the busy classroom teacher will find that these books also serve their needs as changes in the nature and pattern of education make the in-service training of experienced teachers more essential than in the past.

The rationale behind the series is that professional courses for teachers require the coverage of a wide variety of subjects in a relatively short time. So the aim of the series is the production of 'easy to read', practical guides to provide the necessary subject background, supported by references to guide and encourage further reading, together with questions and/or exercises devised to assist application and evaluation.

As specialists in their selected fields, the authors have been chosen for their ability to relate their subjects to the needs of teachers and to stimulate discussion of contemporary issues in education.

The series covers subjects ranging from *'The Theory of Education'* to *'The Teaching of Mathematics'* and from *'Primary School Teaching and Educational Psychology'* to *'Effective Teaching with Information Technology'*. It will look at aspects of education as diverse as *'Education and Cultural Diversity'* and *'Pupil Welfare and Counselling'*. Although some titles, such as *'The Legal Context of Teaching'* and *'The Teaching of History'* are specific to England and Wales, the majority, including *'Assessment in Education'*, *'The Effective Teaching of Statistics'* and *'Comparative Education'*, are international in scope.

Elizabeth Perrott

AUTHOR'S PREFACE

The 1980s saw far-reaching changes in the education system in Britain. While the introduction of the National Curriculum and local management of schools in the 1988 Education Reform Act had the greatest impact on school and classroom practice, the Education Acts of 1980, 1981 and 1986 each placed additional demands on teachers. One of the few things that successive Secretaries of State for Education and Science had in common with most teachers was a desire to raise educational standards. The legislative framework within which schools operate can facilitate or impede this goal, but the full effects of the 1988 Act, for better or worse, will probably not be evident until we are nearly at the next millennium.

Nevertheless, it is quite clear that educational standards are not raised simply by ministerial, nor even parliamentary diktat. They are raised by teachers who have a clear understanding, (a) of the varying influences on children's development both in school and outside it, and (b) of the processes which help children develop into effective, active learners, increasingly willing to undertake intellectually challenging tasks and increasingly able to take responsibility for much of their own learning. The rationale for this book is that educational psychology makes an important contribution in each respect. In other words we aim to show how the psychology of education extends our understanding of teachers' day-to-day work in the classroom as well as of children with particular problems.

In writing the book we took a broad view of what constitutes educational psychology. Thus, we refer to research from developmental, social and clinical psychology where this has obvious implications for the world of the school. For the same reason we make no apology for giving prominence to work on classroom interaction that falls into the grey area between the psychology and the sociology of education.

Our overriding consideration, though, was that the book should address the immediate concerns of primary school teachers. It should stand or fall by the extent to which it recognises their concerns and helps teachers to make sense of their work with children. Educational psychology no longer enjoys its former prominent place in initial teacher training. This is partly the result of changes in teacher training imposed by the government. It is also the result of widespread and entirely legitimate dissatisfaction with much of what has in the past been taught in the name of educational psychology. In particular, we aimed to avoid three common criticisms:

1. Many books, and the courses on which they were used, were over-theoretical, with insufficient links between theory and classroom practice. Consequently they did little to extend teachers' understanding of their own work in the classroom.
2. Few books, if any, have made any serious attempt to identify the common ground between educational psychology and other disciplines, such as the sociology and philosophy of education.
3. There was often an over-emphasis on the psychology of the individual child, with a correspondingly inadequate attention to children's learning in the social context of the classroom.

If our book was to be useful, we believed it would have to avoid a 'Cook's Tour' approach to educational psychology, with its comprehensive but necessarily superficial itinerary through all the main centres of influence. A consequence of this decision was that it demanded an inevitably idiosyncratic selection of the work of psychologists which seemed to us of greatest importance for teachers. In particular, four themes recur throughout the book:

1. the varied and interacting influences of home, the extended family, the school and the classroom (among others) on children's development;
2. the interactive nature of teaching, and the ways in which teachers and children affect each other's behaviour;
3. the importance, both for teachers and for children, of 'metacognitive' skills, i.e. the ability to reflect on the nature of a task, to recognise the demands it makes and to identify appropriate ways of overcoming them;
4. the links between educational psychology and other disciplines.

The final point deserves further explanation. The interests of psychologists do not arise purely from the disinterested pursuit of knowledge. They are grounded in philosophical views of the aims of education and the nature of childhood. Further, many of the concerns of educational psychologists are shared by sociologists. We aim to make these links explicit.

Scope of the book

Educational psychology contains two related but oddly independent traditions. First, the principal concern of educational psychologists employed by LEAs is to provide guidance and advice about the education of children with special educational needs. Their principal concern is with children who for some reason have been identified as problems. Second, academic psychologists have been more concerned, at least recently, with classroom interaction and with the processes involved in effective teaching and learning. Their starting point is the 'normal' classroom. This second tradition is sometimes known as the psychology of education, to distinguish its principal focus from that of educational psychologists. We do not find this distinction helpful. We regard the two traditions as complementary and draw on both in the course of the book.

After an introductory chapter, Chapter 2 examines contextual influences on teachers' understanding of children and on children's own development. This leads into Chapter 3 which reviews recent thinking about provision for children with special educational needs, especially learning and behavioural difficulties. Because the needs of these children cannot be seen in isolation from those of all other children in the class, Chapter 4 considers recent work on classroom interaction. Chapter 5 analyses the ways in which teachers and pupils can make sense of their experience in school and Chapter 6 approaches the vexed issue of classroom management from the position that effective management of behaviour is inextricably linked to management of learning through the curriculum. Because teachers and parents regard schools as having responsibilities which extend beyond the national curriculum, Chapter 7 focuses on personal and social development. Chapter 8 draws together the themes of assessment and evaluation that have been introduced in previous chapters. The final chapter provides an overview and discusses a model for professional development.

Using the book

Each chapter is followed by suggestions for further reading and seminar activities. The book is designed for use by practising primary school teachers and by students on BEd and PGCE courses. It is intended to contribute to teachers' and students' professional awareness. Ideally, professional studies are integrated into the individual's own experience in the classroom. The seminar suggestions indicate some of the ways this can be achieved. Our broader aims are, (a) to encourage people to review and evaluate their own experience as teachers and as learners, and (b) to arouse an interest in ways that educational psychology and other disciplines, contribute to an understanding of effective teaching and learning. The book could be evaluated by the quality of discussion it provokes. As Margaret Sutherland said in her preface to the first volume in this series '*Theory of Education*', we are sorry we shall be unable to take part in the discussion.

David Galloway and Anne Edwards
January 1990

ACKNOWLEDGEMENTS

We are grateful to the numerous students and teachers who have criticised, modified and helped to develop our thinking. Parts of Chapters 2 and 7 are reproduced from David Galloway's book *Pupil Welfare and Counselling* (Longman, 1990).

The publishers are grateful to the following for permission to reproduce copyright material:
Harper Collins Publishers for table 1.1 adapted from Motivation and Personality, 2nd Edition, by Abraham H. Maslow. Copyright 1970 by Abraham H. Maslow; Open books for table 2.1 from School Matters: The Junior Years by P. Mortimore, P. Sammons, G. Stoll and D. Lewis, 1988.

DISCLAIMERS

The views expressed in this book are the authors' own and should not be taken to reflect those of their employers, nor of individuals or institutions who cooperated with any of the inquiries referred to in the book.   When presenting case histories and when quoting teachers or pupils verbatim we have changed names, abbreviations of names, nicknames and other identifying characteristics.

NOTE ON AUTHORSHIP

Planning and writing this book was a cooperative venture. Inevitably, though, there was some division of responsibilities. Each chapter went through at least two drafts as we took account of each other's criticisms. For the record, Chapters 1–3, 7 and 9 were written mainly by David Galloway, and Chapters 4–6 and 8 mainly by Anne Edwards.

DEDICATION

This book is dedicated to our long-suffering families.

LIST OF FIGURES AND TABLES

CHAPTER 1

Getting started: understanding children's needs

Introduction

It is difficult to talk for long about teaching, educational psychology or any other work with children without thinking about their personal, social and educational needs. Indeed professionals working with children exist to meet their presumed needs. Parents, too, often agonise over what would be best for one or more of their children. Yet there is no more agreement about the nature of the needs of primary school children than about the needs of any other age-group. Different people emphasise the importance of different needs, depending not on any absolute psychological or educational truths but on their own background and priorities. Thus one of Her Majesty's Inspectors of schools (HMI) might talk about the need for a 'broad and balanced' curriculum, a child psychiatrist about the need for teachers to provide their more vulnerable pupils with a warm, supportive relationship, and a politician, with an eye on the law and order vote, about the need for discipline.

This book is about the application of psychology, and in particular educational psychology, in primary schools. It assumes that ideas developed by educational psychologists have some value in helping teachers to understand children's needs. Yet teachers could reasonably claim to be bewildered by the range of needs they are expected to meet. They could also claim that the concept of need is itself hopelessly confused. For example when adults say that children *need* affection, do they mean that parents *ought* to show affection, that children have a *right* to affection, that this is a universal psychological *requirement*, or all three? This chapter will examine what we mean when talking about children's needs. We shall then look at two ways of understanding children's needs and finally consider their relevance for infant and junior school teachers.

What do we mean when talking about children's needs?

Since the 1988 Education Reform Act Britain has had provision for a National Curriculum. This summarises what the Department of

Education and Science (DES) thinks children need to, or should, learn in the years of compulsory education. The National Curriculum represents one view of children's needs. Another 'official' view is represented in the Teachers' Conditions of Service document (DES,1988a) which requires teachers to have regard to pupils 'general progress and well-being'. Clearly, this implies that teachers' responsibilities for their pupils extend beyond the curriculum to include their welfare or pastoral needs.

This is all pretty remote, though, from the concerns of parents as their children start school at the age of 4 or 5. Parents may initially define their children's needs in terms such as: (a) being happy at school; (b) feeling cared for, secure, looked after; (c) making friends; (d) learning 'good' behaviour and attitudes; (e) making progress in the '3 Rs', if not in other areas of the National Curriculum.

Yet even this is pretty remote from the immediate needs both of children and of teachers as children start school. To see other ways of defining children's needs we have only to ask what their own and their teachers' first impressions may be at the start of the year. Children's first impression are likely to depend largely on the familiarity of the new environment. In turn this may depend on whether they have visited the school previously and met their teacher, whether a parent stops with them for part or all of the first few days, whether they already know other children, whether they know where to hang their coat, where to go at play-time, where the loos are, and so on. In other words their immediate needs are for security and stability. How far these needs are met will depend partly on the school's policy, partly on the individual teacher and partly on their parents.

Our own children attended six different infant schools. At one of these all parents were expected to visit the school with their child and to spend time with them in the classroom. At three this was accepted though not actively encouraged; at a fifth it was tolerated but discouraged, and at the sixth a hand-written notice at the entrance from the playground proclaimed: No Parents Beyond This Point. Significantly, this notice was largely ignored by the minority of middle-class parents but successfully intimidated the majority from working-class and ethnic minority groups. Thus *all* children learned that parents varied in their power to provide security.

Teachers too, have an obvious need for stability and security. At the start of the year their priority is not just to get to know the children. They have to observe whether children appear used to working and playing together, or seem alert, interested and keen to take part while others are identified as needing a close eye kept on them, because they do not follow instructions, appear tearful, or quarrel with other children. In other words, teachers' immediate priorities are with classroom organisation and management as well as with the learning activities they aim to provide.

In all this, teachers are using their professional knowledge to formulate and test theories about children and groups of children. They may not do this consciously, but teaching cannot take place without assessment, and assessment takes place at several different levels (see Chapter 8). Children lack professional knowledge but they too are starting to 'weigh up' their teacher and other aspects of the classroom environment: 'What happens if I go on playing in the home corner when she says it's time for lunch? What happened when Jamie threw some water on the floor?'

Children's own answers to their questions will influence their perception of the classroom, whether they feel it is a safe, interesting, happy place to be, or unpredictable and unfriendly. For teachers the position is more complex. Their sense of security will be affected by a variety of factors, varying from the nature of their contract, the quality of support from the head and from colleagues, and the amount of resources available. It is also affected by their own success in classroom organisation and management. This is partly a question of organising the available resources in a way that arouses the children's interest and partly of organising the children themselves so that they benefit from the learning experiences provided. Failure on either count will be evident in the children's behaviour, as they feel increasingly unsettled, restless and unsure of themselves. Teachers depend for their job satisfaction and their self-esteem on seeing children making progress within the classroom environment they have created. It follows, that there is a close relationship between teachers' definition of their pupils' needs and the needs of teachers themselves.

Needs, wants and rights

Teachers identify children's needs informally through discussions with each other and by developing their own categorisation systems. These are no different in quality from the informal categorisations used in any social relationships and may identify children in terms such as 'bright', 'disruptive', 'difficult home', 'needs watching' and so on. In the same way, people may classify their neighbours by occupation, by hobby, by political inclination, by whether they have children, by the behaviour of their children ('the ones with the whining 2 year-old') or by whether they are interesting to talk to.

Teachers also use more formal procedures to define children's needs, ranging from hearing them read, to administering standardised tests purporting to measure intelligence and educational attainment. Clearly these are assessment techniques as well as aids to identifying and understanding children's needs. The point is that logically we cannot talk about children's needs not being met without having first made an assessment that they lack something important to their development. Similarly, in claiming that we are meeting a child's needs we claim that we are providing the things we consider important to his or her development.

The important issue here is that the things a teacher considers most important to a child's development may not coincide with what the child's parent considers most important. Different people give priority to different needs. This is partly a matter of professional affiliation. Teachers can no longer work in isolation, if indeed this was ever the case. They are accountable to their head teacher, and through the head to the school's governors and to their employers, all of whom have more or less clear expectations as to what pupils should be achieving at school. Some of these expectations are now enshrined in a national curriculum. Inevitably they affect how teachers define children's needs. Other professionals such as social workers or doctors have different responsibilities and are accountable to other bodies. Consequently they define children's needs in different terms. Thus, a social worker might emphasise the importance of parenting in the early years, while a social psychologist might be concerned foremost with the child's developing awareness of being part of a social community.

In each case the assessment of what children need is based on what the person concerned 'wants' for the child. It also implies that the person thinks that children have a right to have their needs met. Hence, in talking about children's needs we are making a value judgement about what *we* think should be provided for children. Unfortunately there are two complicating factors here:

1. There is no agreement within the teaching profession, nor between teachers, other professionals or the government on what constitute children's rights. In passing the 1988 Education Reform Act the government implicitly stated that parents have a right to know what their children will be taught. The introduction of the National Curriculum reflected the government's assessment that schools were providing an inadequate education for a very large minority of pupils. In claiming that educational provision was inadequate, the government was making a value judgement. Virtually all teacher associations disputed this value judgement, and consequently saw no need for a national curriculum. Teachers, parents or government committees may claim a 'scientific' basis for their concerns about children's needs, as in the Warnock Committee's, claim that 20 per cent of pupils may be expected to require some form of special educational help at some stage in their school career (DES, 1978a, see Chapter 3). Ultimately, though, these claims come down to a value judgement on the part of the individuals or groups concerned. This is no criticism. Teaching is not value free and never can be. Moreover, as public employees, teachers are accountable to parents, governors and employees, and consequently cannot have complete autonomy in defining children's needs.

2. The second problem is more complex. Teaching is a social activity, and teachers are accountable for the behaviour and progress of the class as a whole. In saying that a boy needs to learn to sit down, or that a girl needs to learn not to shout out, teachers are likely to be making a statement about their own need for control as much as about the child's need to learn an important social skill. This problem becomes even more acute in the case of children whose behaviour or educational progress gives cause for exceptional concern. The problem may lie in the resources available in the classroom, in the methods the teacher is using, or in the overall management and organisation of the classroom. The temptation, though, will be to define the problem in terms of the needs of an individual child or group of children. In other words needs are individualised: the child is said to have special needs as a way of avoiding recognition of the professional needs of the teacher. There are two implications. First, children's needs have to be seen in the context of the classroom and of the school. Secondly, if children are thought to have special needs, or even ordinary needs which are not adequately being met, this may have implications for the resources available to teachers and/or for their teaching methods.

Can we talk about 'psychological' needs?

We believe that educational psychology does have some value in helping teachers to understand their own experience in school and also that of their pupils, even though changes in teacher training have unseated it from the central position it once held (DES, 1989a). This is quite different, however, from claiming that it is possible to identify psychological needs as opposed to personal, social or educational ones. A conventional definition of psychology is the study of behaviour. We cannot talk about personal, social or educational needs without implying that we think children or people in their environment should behave in certain ways. Even if we define psychology as the study of the mind, it is logically impossible to think of psychological needs which do not imply some form of behaviour. The behaviour may not be directly observable, for example, thinking or reflection, but it is still behaviour.

Psychologists live and work in a social world as well as observing it. Unfortunately, they sometimes make the mistake of trying to identify children's needs in isolation, away from the context in which they are living, working and playing. It does not follow, however, that needs identified in the course of an educational psychologist's one-to-one interview with a child can usefully be described as psychological needs. The reason is simply that any identified needs will have implications for the child's future behaviour and, almost certainly, for that of teachers or parents. It follows that the needs identified by psychologists, like those identified by teachers, imply an interaction between children and the people in their environment.

Two ways of thinking about children's needs

A hierarchy of needs?

Maslow (1970) argued that people have a hierarchy of needs from the basic needs for food and drink to 'self-actualisation' or the sense of self-fulfillment that comes from achieving one's full potential. This hierarchy is summarised in Table 1.1. Maslow argued that people are only motivated to achieve higher level needs when lower level needs have been met. In fact this is not always the case.

Table 1.1 **Summary of Maslow's Hierarchy of Needs**

Highest Level :	'Self-actualisation'; the sense of self-fulfilment that comes from achieving one's full potential.
	Aesthetic appreciation
	Intellectual challenge and achievement
	Self-esteem: the need for approval and recognition
	Sense of belonging/membership of family, class, peer group
	Safety: the need to feel physically and psychologically secure
Lowest Level :	Survival: basic needs for food, drink, etc.

Adapted from Maslow (1970)

Neither children nor adults always progress up the hierarchy in an orderly way. For example, primary children who place themselves in dangerous situations, for example walking across an electrified railway line or, more conventionally, seeing who can climb to the highest point of a tree, may be placing their need for approval and recognition from other children before the need to feel 'physically and psychologically secure'. Nevertheless, two examples will illustrate how failure to meet lower-order needs on Maslow's hierarchy may affect pupils' progress, resulting in frustration for pupil and teacher alike. In both cases no amount of curriculum development or attention to teaching methods would have made much difference.

1. Jenny frequently had a runny nose. In the infants school a box of tissues was an indispensable part of her teacher's classroom equipment. She was described as being 'in a world of her own' and had a reputation for not listening to instructions. She had to be told everything twice. When she was 9 her mother took her to the

doctor because she was unusually 'chesty'. The doctor confirmed that she had an infection, but also diagnosed catarrhal deafness, often known as 'glue ear', associated with colds, minor infections and hay fever. There were times when she had no hearing loss. Yet her tendency to 'switch off' rather than concentrate in order to hear what the teacher said, continued even when she was physically fit. Since she started school her education had been affected by her hearing loss. By the time it was diagnosed, secondary problems of loss of motivation had developed.

2. The third and fourth year classes in a senior school were based in terrapins in the school playground and had a long-standing reputation for being hard to teach. When they moved classrooms and left the terrapins teachers noticed after a few weeks that they had become much easier. Three years earlier a teacher had complained about the noise and flicker from the ancient strip-lights in the terrapins. The head had forwarded the complaint to County Hall but nothing had been done and the head had not persisted.

Maslow's hierarchy has limited usefulness as a psychological theory: people do not always behave in the ways it predicts. Nevertheless, it does illustrate the complex interrelationships involved in teaching. As both vignettes show, effective teaching cannot take place without attention to aspects of pupil welfare. Indeed, the interrelationship between teaching and welfare becomes even more evident when we consider the fourth need on Maslow's hierarchy, self-esteem.

Teachers can infer low esteem from children's reluctance to attempt something they may find difficult, from observing them to be fearful in new situations, from disparaging remarks they make about their own work, or from their general relationships with other children. Superficially the explanation may appear obvious, for example that the child has a minor physical disability, is 'slower' than other children educationally, or is constantly being compared with a more successful older brother or sister at home. Yet a commitment to pupils' personal, social and educational welfare will lead us to reject such explanations, or at least to look beyond them. Thus, how pupils with asthma or some other physical impairment see themselves may depend largely on how successfully their infant or junior school teachers create a climate which accepts and respects individual differences. Many parents recall their child coming home from infants' school with the news that she or he has been moved up a table. (Children do not always report it when they think they have been moved down.) Even at this age children can equate ability with status, and it may be the feeling that they have been labelled 'slow' rather than the low attainment as such which negatively affects their motivation.

Even when a child is under pressure due to home circumstances much can depend on how the school interprets the situation. Both of us have heard teachers in infant schools talking within children's hearing about their difficult home circumstances. Even when the discussion is not within the children's hearing they are often quick to sense their teachers' judgements. Schools vary widely in their success in establishing active and constructive contacts with their pupils' parents. There is now extensive evidence of the lasting benefits of parental involvement in children's early years at school, much of it from research carried out in economically disadvantaged inner-city areas (e.g. Tizard, Schofield and Hewison, 1982). When teachers succeed in conveying to children that they regard their parents as important people in their lives, rather than as the source of their problems, the impact on the children's self-esteem is likely to be profound and lasting.

Maslow's hierarchy of needs implicitly emphasises the importance of adults recognising and meeting children's needs. Obviously, teachers have to make assessments about their pupils' needs, but this should not obscure the fact that teaching is an inter-active process to which children also contribute. The fact that the teacher is responsible for the classroom's stability and that the child has to learn to work and play with other children suggest another way of looking at children's needs.

Schooling as a process of adaption

Meeting the needs of children is not simply a case of predicting or responding to the demands of pupils. The reality is far more complex. First one purpose of schooling is to create citizens, skilled members of society. To that extent the needs of children may be defined by external forces rather than by schools. Teachers are themselves therefore severely constrained in the ways they are able to define, recognise and react to needs.

The perception of the child's need as either appropriate or inappropriate may well depend upon the 'climate' of the school. Galloway and Goodwin (1987) describe school climate as a network of relationships between pupils and teachers 'that determines what they expect of each other'. Climates vary and hence recognition of, and responses to needs differ. The importance of climate to the development of a child as pupil and as citizen is highlighted by a perspective on child development provided by Shotter (1984). Borrowing a metaphor from ecology, he describes childhood itself as a 'niche' provided by society in which the child is allowed to develop. That niche helps to shape the child into the fully developed model of adulthood appropriate to a particular society. The child in turn may act on the niche to modify it and hence its expectations or developmental opportunities. However, when Shotter's framework is applied to schooling it could be argued that there are considerable external pressures on the niche itself which inhibit any flexibility it might wish to have in responding to all the needs of pupils. Schools as niches which turn children into pupils are both constraining and constrained.

Taking this argument a stage further, Willes (1981) provides interesting insights into the processes of 'pupil-making' in her analysis of classroom talk in reception classes. She observes how children are turned into pupils during their early experiences of classroom life. She notes that children learn how to operate within the expectations held of appropriate classroom behaviour, despite receiving very little formal instruction to that end. A method frequently used by reception class teachers is to behave 'as if' children understand the rules of behaviour and know how to engage in classroom life. Consequently teachers are able to keep the dominant role and children are socialised, through the lenient interpretation of their behaviour by teachers, into becoming participating pupils. Willes makes one salutary observation; 'To be a fully participating pupil is not necessarily to be an independent and well motivated learner' (Willes, 1981, p. 61).

To this the response of teachers can only be that the converse, equally, is not necessarily the case. Two of the themes explored in this volume relate to ways in which children may become increasingly in control of their own learning processes and the importance of a sense of effectiveness and motivation to the success of that endeavour. That this is to be achieved within the constraints operating in schools as providers of 'schooling' means that any examination of children in schools needs to take the context of their behaviours or experiences into full consideration.

Relevance for infant and junior school teachers

We have outlined three ways of thinking about children's needs in the classroom. How, in their different ways, do Maslow, Shotter and Willes help teachers to recognise the varying influences on children's experience in the classroom, and indeed on their own? One answer is suggested from research on effective teaching. This suggests that children can acquire the skill of 'metacognition', or the ability to monitor the demands of a task and to take appropriate action to solve problems they encounter. In other words, children have learned to recognise when they find a task difficult and to work out why. They may seek help from the teacher or they may have learned how to find a solution for themselves. In either case they are starting to become autonomous, since they are not solely dependent on the teacher for approval or guidance. By thinking about, or reflecting on, what they are doing, they are learning how to learn. Two examples illustrate this process.

1. James has started a jigsaw. He has fitted a quarter of the pieces together, but is now stuck. He shuffles the pieces around, apparently trying to fix them together at random. Eventually he moves off to another task leaving the uncompleted puzzle. John arrives at the table: 'let's finish it'. He looks at the picture then at the completed part of the puzzle: 'dog . . . now sky . . . where's the blue pieces?' A friend joins him and they talk about the parts of the picture they are looking for, the colours, the shapes of the pieces and what sort of piece they need next. They correct each other as they go along. Soon, the puzzle is finished and they show it to their teacher.

2. Jenny's group of 10–11 year olds is working on a project on commercial uses of timber. Their task is to find out about woods used in furniture making in Britain. They are referred to a book to start them off but after looking at this they go back to their teacher for another suggestion. This time they are told to see what they can find in an encyclopaedia. Again they return to the teacher for help. In the next-door class Sharon is working on the same project, with the task of finding out as much as she can about the uses of trees in making paper. She starts with the class book shelves, but knows that she will find out more in another room where reference books are kept. These direct her to other sources and she calls in at the public library on the way home. She writes to the Canadian High Commission and to the embassies of other countries for information about paper manufacture. Soon she is relating all this to conservation and re-cycling.

Metacognitive skills do not just develop. They are learned from observation of other children, from the way the teachers organise children's learning and from the nature of feedback they give children. Teaching is not only about the transmission of facts and never has been. It is also concerned with teaching children how to learn. An essential element in this is the ability to monitor what they are doing, and to adapt their strategies in the light of this.

Perhaps the most important function of theory in education is to help teachers acquire the metacognitive skill they wish to develop in their pupils. Theories, then, are useful if they help teachers to reflect on their own practice, and to evaluate it. Monitoring one's own teaching cannot be divorced from monitoring the children's progress. It implies that the climate and organisation of the classroom and everything else in the nebulous but important concept of teaching quality, will affect their development.

A theory should do more, however, than help teachers to reflect on and to evaluate their own practice. It should also give them the ability, or power, to modify or develop their classroom practice. In other words theories are useful if teachers can use them to generate and test theories of their own. Teaching can be seen as a constant process of generating and testing ideas, or theories about children's knowledge, understanding, skills, attitudes and behaviour. Understandably, teachers repeat strategies that have proved successful in the past. Often these have been discovered by a lengthy process of trial and error, which is a notoriously inefficient way of learning. Also, some teachers have blind spots about important aspects of their pupils' development. The work of psychologists, as of educational sociologists, historians and philosophers can be seen as an aid to monitoring and evaluating their own experience and thereby exploring ways of improving it.

Conclusions

How a person defines children's needs will depend on that person's background and priorities as much as on the children themselves. Moreover, it makes no sense to talk about children's needs in isolation from the context in which they are living, working and playing. In this chapter we have looked at two ways of making sense of children's needs in infant and junior schools and have related these to the importance for teachers of monitoring and evaluating their own work. One assumption throughout the chapter has been that teaching is a social activity. Hence we must now turn to ways of thinking about the complex interactions that take place in all classrooms.

Notes and further reading

1. For a discussion of the interrelationships in children's educational, personal and social development see: Galloway, D. (1990) *Pupil Welfare and Counselling: An Approach to Personal and Social Education Across the Curriculum.* London, Longman (Effective Teacher Series).
2. Teachers work within a legislative framework. Their perceptions of the impact of recent legislation are also likely to affect their underlying sense of security. For a useful discussion of the 1988 Education Reform Act, see: McClure, S. (1989) *Education Reformed.* London, Hodder and Stoughton. A more sharply critical view is given by: Simon, B. (1989) *The Great Schooling Scandal.* London, Lawrence and Wishart.
3. The Council for Accreditation of Teacher Education (CATE) has produced a set of criteria which all initial teacher training courses are required to satisfy. See DES (1989). For a discussion of the controversies surrounding psychology's contribution to education, see: Claxton, G., Swann, W., Salmon, P., Walkerdine, V., Jacobsen, B. and White, J. (1985) Psychology and Schooling: What's the matter? Bedford Way Paper, 25. London, University of London Institute of Education.

4. An excellent introduction to the theory of education is provided by:
    Sutherland, M. (1988) *Theory of Education*. London, Longman (Effective Teacher Series).
    For two more general books relating theoretical perspectives to classroom practice, see:
    Cohen, L. and Marion, L. (1981) *Perspectives on Classrooms and Schools*. London, Holt, Rinehart and Winston.
    Woolfolk, A.E. and Nicolich, C.M. (1980) *Educational Psychology for Teachers*. Englewood Cliffs NJ, Prentice-Hall.

Seminar suggestions

1. Examine the prospectus for each school in which members of the group have most recently worked. Do they differ in the way they talk about children's needs?
2. From the perspective of militant members of each of the two main political parties, write entries on the psychological needs of children for a school prospectus. Consider the different priorities that emerge from this exercise, and discuss how far Maslow's hierarchy of needs has a 'political' or ideological basis.
3. Drawing on Shotter's concept of childhood as an ecological 'niche', write a short (up to one page) account of one child's adaption to a new school/class. Compare different accounts, and consider: (a) how the child was helped/encouraged to adapt to the requirements of the classroom: (b) whether the child succeeded in modifying the classroom in any way.

CHAPTER 2

Similarities and differences

Introduction

Priorities and values

Educational psychology in Britain has been preoccupied with individual differences since Cyril Burt became the then London County Council's first educational psychologist in 1913. How we think about individual differences depends on what we believe an education service should be providing, how we view a state's responsibility to its citizens and vice versa. In other words it depends on our priorities and values.

Let us start by considering a conventional argument. If teachers claim to be meeting the needs of individual pupils they must necessarily have an interest in individual differences, unless they believe, naively, that all pupils are the same. If educational psychologists aim to help teachers meet their pupils' needs, they too must have an interest in individual differences. This argument appears so eminently reasonable as hardly to be worth stating. In fact, it *is* eminently reasonable if we accept the premise on which it is based, namely that teachers *are* trying to meet the needs of all their pupils. After all, if pupils are not all the same, as they manifestly are not, it would surely be grossly unfair to teach them all in exactly the same way. An awareness of individual differences will merely help teachers to see how to adapt the curriculum to the needs of the child.

Unfortunately, the premise is contentious. As we shall argue throughout this book, teachers are not free agents. They are accountable to their colleagues, the school governors, their pupils' parents and to the pupils themselves. Moreover neither teacher nor pupils start the school year with a *tabula rasa*: they have all come to internalise certain beliefs, values and prejudices which will influence how they think about individual differences and how they behave towards each other. These constitute the hidden agenda, or unstated reasons for an interest in individual differences. We consider four arguments below:

1. Categorising pupils by ability, behaviour or gender is an organisational convenience. Boys and girls can be lined up separately, the 'slow' readers can be seated together, as can the difficult trio who need a constant eye keeping on them.
2. Categorising pupils legitimises the teacher's own preconceptions about the groups concerned: 'Boys are always noisy; girls can be so spiteful to each other'; 'We mustn't expect too much as we know all about the home background'; 'He can't read because he's dyslexic'; 'Black children are often rowdy'. The expected ability and behaviour of boys/girls, ethnic minority pupils, pupils with professional parents or pupils with special needs can form part of any teacher's or psychologist's personal value system. By organising a class around recognition of such differences we are merely creating the conditions which reinforce this value system, or to put it another way, which strengthen our prejudices and thereby remove any need to confront and question them.
3. Categorising pupils enables us to remove them from the classroom by shunting them into a low status siding which is then legitimised as intending to meet their special needs (see Chapter 3). In infant and junior schools this happens when a part-time teacher is allocated to special needs and removes children for extra help which bears little or no relationship to what the rest of the class is doing. It also happens when children are removed by members of LEA reading and language services.
4. By focusing on differences we remove the perhaps uncomfortable necessity to recognise what children have in common, and hence to review our teaching methods and classroom organisation, to consider how we can cater for the *similarities* between them rather than the differences.

Conflicts between aims?

Helping children achieve their 'full potential' is an explicit aim in most school prospectuses and staff handbooks. Since this apparently uncontroversial aim is so ubiquitous, it is interesting that the Conservative government of the 1980s was so vocal in denouncing the alleged underachievement of academically less able pupils. Indeed at the height of the worst recession since the 1930s the Secretary of State was able to secure funds to launch the 'Lower Attaining Pupil Programme' (Joseph, 1983), a stunningly uninspired title which could only have been dreamed up by a civil servant or by a politician with no expectation that the beneficiaries would ever consider voting for his party.

At least since the Plowden Report (CACE, 1967), primary teachers have insisted on the intrinsically worthwhile nature of education.

Obviously, it is important to prepare children for their junior or secondary school, but the real purpose of education is to give them intrinsically worthwhile experiences *now*. During the 1980s this liberal view of the aims of education came under attack. Education was increasingly seen as an instrument of government policy, with an emphasis on teachers' responsibility for equipping pupils with the knowledge, skills and attitudes that would enable them to meet the changing demands of the labour market and to play a 'responsible' role in society.

At first some primary teachers thought this changing climate would only affect secondary schools. It soon became clear that they were not exempt. Students leaving initial teacher training courses were required to be able to teach children about industry and the world of work (DES, 1989a), HMI took an increasingly critical interest in the role of post-holders with designated responsibility for specific curriculum areas (DES, 1978b). The curriculum itself underwent substantial change, with the introduction of science and technology and, following the 1988 Education Reform Act, the national curriculum.

The consultations that took place before the 1988 Act was laid before Parliament showed massive professional opposition (Haviland, 1988). Teachers clearly not only disliked the proposals in the Act, but also mistrusted the government's increasingly instrumentalist approach to education. They argued:

1. that the national testing programme associated with the National Curriculum would label large numbers of children as failures from the age of 7;
2. that pressure of national testing would lead to selection within schools, with the best teachers being allocated to the brightest children, as in the days of the 11+;
3. that giving parents greater freedom to choose their child's school would create ghetto schools of disadvantaged pupils, especially in urban areas in which parents could not afford to send their children to more privileged schools in the proverbial leafy suburbs;
4. that grant-maintained schools would further accelerate this process;
5. that under local financial management of schools, head teachers and governors would be unwilling to allocate funds to pupils with exceptional needs.

Thus, the objections to the innovations of the 1980s were based largely on the assumption that they would accentuate divisions within the school system and increase the pressure on teachers to differentiate between children in educationally and socially undesirable ways. Far from helping teachers to meet children's needs the Acts of 1980, 1986 and 1988 would make it virtually impossible for teachers to avoid creating them.

These objections raise two issues. First, it is not yet clear whether the 1988 Act will result in discrimination against disadvantaged pupils. Elsewhere I have argued with tongue only partly in cheek that it could be seen as a Marxist measure (Galloway, 1990). Secondly, it is not at all clear that the rhetoric of the liberal view of education was ever justified. This rhetoric was derived from the dominant individualistic value system of teaching and educational psychology. It claimed to help all pupils achieve their full potential; by concentrating on the individual's needs, potentially destructive comparisons between children could be avoided. This view deserves closer attention.

Why do children fail and is it inevitable?

We cannot fail at a task unless we have set out to complete it. We may set ourselves the task, or have been set it by someone else. The effect of failure depends on how it is perceived by the child, peers, teachers and other people such as parents. Children learn very quickly that some tasks are valued more highly than others. Not many infant or junior school children are referred to educational psychologists because of their teacher's or parent's deep concern about their difficulties with painting or modelling. Lack of progress in language, reading and mathematics is a different matter altogether. Whether lack of success, or more bluntly, failure, matters, depends largely on the status of the task.[1]

Consider two children, William and Joanne entering the reception class of an infant school. Initially their principal task is to adapt to classroom routine. They will notice whether or not their teacher is pleased, whether or not she is concerned. As they become socialised into the routine of the classroom they will become aware that some activities are considered more important than others. This is a gradual process, but an inexorable one. William may notice that the teacher is pleased with his paintings, but concerned about his lack of interest in maths. Joanne may notice that everyone is enthusiastic about her singing and enjoyment of music, but worried about her lack of progress in reading. Over a period of time, perhaps years, both children will realise that their own lack of progress in these core subjects appears more important both to their teachers and to their parents than other children's difficulties with painting or music.

This is the process to which sociologists are referring when they say that the status of knowledge is 'socially created'. What neither William nor Joanne can recognise is that the status accorded different forms of knowledge varies over time. Difficulties with reading and mathematics still attract more concern than any other curriculum area, but ability in the creative arts is probably valued more highly today than it would have been in the 1930s, or even 1950s. Similarly, oral skills are probably valued more highly in 1990 than was the case as little as ten years earlier.

Children's awareness of the importance of different tasks develops as part of their socialisation in the home, and continues at school. By the time they start school they will have 'learned' gender-specific roles; part of this learning is that boys need some skills more than girls, and vice versa. We may accept that this learning occurs and even welcome it, or we may deplore it and do everything possible to counteract it, but the evidence that it takes place is hardly contentious. Similarly, children in families with a lot of books will have learned the importance, and probably enjoyment, of reading, while others will have had little experience with books but have developed skills in working with tools and making things.

It follows that in starting school some tasks may appear more relevant to a child than others. This becomes a problem when the tasks the teacher considers important are felt by the child to be unimportant. By the time they move to their junior school children have developed a reasonably clear idea of what their teachers and their parents consider important. They are also developing powers of 'metaperception', or the ability to recognise what other people think about them. This can have unfortunate consequences as when children live down to the expectation of a parent or teacher that they are 'not as quick' as an older brother or sister.

Although what counts as high status is culturally determined, the existence of status is evident in all cultures. Whether it is conferred by birth, by membership of a particular tribe or caste, by possession of certain kinds of knowledge or skill, by sporting or literary prowess or by acquired wealth will depend on the dominant values held in society at a given stage in its history. The idea of total equality is naive. Irrespective of the dominant ideology, certain individuals and groups have the power to make decisions affecting the lives of others. Indeed if this were not the case there would be anarchy.

We seem to be reaching a depressingly gloomy conclusion that some pupils must inevitably be disadvantaged by low status. So far, however, we have skated over a distinction which suggests a way round this problem. Power and status are not synonymous. In Britain the royal family has high status, but very little real power. Estate agents, have the power which comes from financial wealth but repeated surveys show that they are not highly regarded by the public at large. The same may apply to accountants and to politicians in local government. One aim of the so-called Thatcherite revolution of the 1980s, was to change the public perception of the creation of wealth. Many people came to regard this as morally desirable, if not to be flaunted, and not, like sex to the Victorians, nasty but necessary with any enjoyment well hidden.

Teachers can do little to influence the importance parents attach to different areas of the curriculum. They can do even less to influence the occupations which bestow power and/or prestige. Yet the fact that power and prestige are *not* the same suggests that teachers *do* have some scope for defining what is morally desirable and worthwhile. A practical example is seen in children's annual reports which distinguish between effort and attainment. There is no logical reason preventing teachers attaching as much value to artistic as to literary achievement, nor in preventing them from valuing the achievements of their academically least able pupils as highly as those of the most able.

Yet we should not underestimate the cultural pressures against such high-sounding rhetoric. The head of an infant school may be able to show publicly that he or she values the effective work of a class teacher with two sight-impaired children who have just arrived in Britain from Pakistan as highly as her work with children with no obvious special needs. As long as the local parents are satisfied with their own children's progress, they may well take pleasure and pride that other children are also doing well. Cultural pressures increase, though, as children get older. Some secondary heads might truthfully be able to say that they value the achievement of a teacher in helping children with severe and complex difficulties to learn to read as highly as that of another teacher in helping three or four pupils win places at Oxbridge. It would be an unusual head who would state this publicly, let alone convince parents and colleagues that he or she really believed it.

Family, school and social class influences on children's educational development

Until the mid-1960s it was widely assumed that family background had the overwhelming influence on children's progress at school.[2] The National Child Development Study followed all children born between 3–9 March 1958 (Wedge and Prosser, 1973; Wedge and Essen, 1982). Children were defined as disadvantaged when their families:

1. had only one parent and/or five or more children;
2. lived in an over-crowded house or a house with no hot water;
3. received means-tested welfare benefits on account of their low income.

The study found a strong and consistent relationship between family disadvantage and low attainment at school. More worrying still, this relationship became more marked as the children grew older.

Other research has similarly emphasised the impact of family factors on pupils' development. Rutter (1966), for example, noted the effect of parental ill-health, and in particular psychiatric ill-health. Galloway (1985) found a very high rate of social disadvantage, combined in many cases with evidence of psychiatric problems in families of children who were persistently absent from school. This was most strikingly evident in the sample of primary pupils. Conversely, children from stable, achievement-oriented families start school with the dual advantages that teachers see their parents as cooperative and also that their parents are able to reinforce at home what they do in school.

There is little doubt, then, that family background exerts an important influence on pupils' progress and adjustment at school. This view lay behind the recommendation of the Plowden Committee on primary education to set up educational priority areas (CACE, 1967). Accepting advice from educationalists and psychologists, the committee believed that a child's progress and social development depended on intelligence, personality and family background. Little could be done about any of these. Moreover, the evidence at the time suggested that individual schools made little difference to their pupils' life chances. How a child got on would depend on constitutional and family factors, not on the school's own policy and practice. Certainly, we cannot ignore the influence of family and community factors on children's educational achievements. Pupils attending inner city schools appear particularly vulnerable (Training Agency, 1990).

Nevertheless it should be recognised that this is an over-simplification, since schools are not all equally effective. Heal (1978) noted substantial differences between primary schools in their pupils' behaviour, and claimed these could not be attributed to their home backgrounds. The following year Rutter *et al.* (1979) published their study of secondary schools and their effects on pupils, claiming that a pupil's examination results, attendance, chances of getting into trouble with the police and behaviour within the school were all influenced by the school they attended as well as by their social background. By far the most important study of primary school effectiveness in Britain, however, remains that of Mortimore *et al.* (1988). Mortimore and his colleagues studied 50 junior schools in Inner London. Over a four-year period they studied the pupils' educational progress (arguing that the school's effect should be measured by the pupils' progress, not by their absolute attainments since the latter varied widely when the pupils entered the school), their self-concept, their attitudes to different school activities, their attendance and their behaviour in school.

It is worth considering why teachers, psychologists and educational researchers had for so long assumed that schools would exert little if any influence on pupils' educational progress and social adjustment independent of their family and social background. The implication of this assumption is extraordinary: namely that all schools are the same, and that a pupil's progress depends principally on factors over which teachers have no control. Few parents have ever believed this, and estate agents frequently advertise houses as being close to a particularly popular school. The school's influence was probably overlooked for three reasons:

1. Educational psychology was for a long time preoccupied with the assessment of intelligence and personality, largely for the purpose of selecting children for special education or for child guidance clinic treatment. This preoccupation saw problems as being located 'in' a child or family and diverted attention from the quality of teaching provided in school.
2. Sociological research emphasised the influence of social class on children's life chances. Teachers saw themselves as members of a middle-class profession and this research may have reinforced a tendency to underestimate the ability of working-class children (see Tizard *et al.* (1988) for evidence that this is the case).
3. Previous research on differences between schools had concentrated on structural factors such as resources, buildings and school size (e.g. CACE, 1967; Coleman *et al.*, 1966). It is now clear that these have relatively little impact on a school's overall effectiveness, at least in Britain. The process of education appears far more important.[3]

What makes a school effective?

Mortimore *et al.* (1988) investigated the policies, practices and organisation of their London junior schools. They identified twelve factors which were evident in the more effective schools but less evident in others (see Table 2.1).

Table 2.1 The twelve key factors making an effective school

---

1. Purposeful leadership of the staff by the head teacher.
2. The involvement of the deputy head.
3. The involvement of teachers.
4. Consistency among teachers.
5. Structured sessions.
6. Intellectually challenging teaching.
7. The work-centred environment.
8. Limited focus within sessions.
9. Maximum communication between teachers and pupils.
10. Record keeping.
11. Parental involvement.
12. Positive climate.

Source: Mortimore *et al.* (1988), p. 250.[4]

The principal problem with this kind of research is that it is essentially descriptive and atheoretical. Both Rutter *et al.* (1979) and Mortimore's team acknowledge that they cannot claim a causal relationship between the factors they identify and a school's effectiveness. Thus Rutter found that pot plants were more in evidence at the effective schools than in less effective ones. Does this mean that pot plants contributed to the positive ethos in these schools, or simply that no pot plants would have survived for long in other schools? Were they a cause or an effect of the school effectiveness? Similarly, Mortimore found the role of the deputy head important. Schools in which the deputy was frequently absent or played little active part tended to have lower pupil performance. Again, we have no way of telling why this might have been the case.

A quite different approach to children's progress through their primary schools has examined the impact of the school on the pupil's development as individuals. Two constraints which are central to a person's concept of self are gender and ethnicity. Do schools provide equality of opportunity for boys and girls and for members of different ethnic groups, or do they accentuate differences?

Other influences on educational development

Gender

Most primary schools would claim to provide equal opportunities for boys and girls. Many teachers go further and insist, indignantly, that 'we treat them both the same'. Clearly, though, teachers' behaviour towards boys and girls is often not the same.[5] There is extensive evidence that teachers report more boys as disruptive than girls (e.g. Rutter, Tizard and Whitmore, 1970), and there is some evidence from independent observations that boys are more likely to behave in 'difficult' ways than girls (e.g. Tizard *et al.* 1988). Again, evidence in Britain shows that boys are more frequently backward in reading than girls (e.g. Rutter, Tizard and Whitmore, 1970).

It is not, however, so clearly the case in Germany (Preston, 1962). This raises interesting questions about how boys come to be identified as disruptive and about why they are more likely in Britain to have learning difficulties. The claim that boys and girls receive the same treatment and opportunities seldom bears close scrutiny. From the moment they enter school gender-linked differences are emphasised in a whole variety of ways, both covert and overt. In a large majority of schools boys and girls hang their coats in different places and boys' names are called before girls when taking the register. In many primary schools boys and girls line up separately to enter and leave the classroom. In some they even sit in different groups for assembly with the threat of being made to sit with the girls (or, less frequently the boys) a powerful sanction against pupils who misbehave. Even if these activities are integrated, few junior school head teachers would dare to integrate the toilets.

The organisational differences may have less impact on pupils than the differences in behaviour expected of boys and girls. Since many teachers are parents, it is not surprising that like parents they often expect boys to be noisier and more rowdy than girls. A girl who prefers to dress like a boy may attract little comment, but a boy who prefers to dress like a girl is often the subject of concern. Behaviour which is labelled 'boisterous' in a boy may be called 'aggressive' in a girl. There is some evidence that teachers tend to attribute girls' failure on a task to lack of ability, whereas boys' failure is more likely to be attributed to lack of effort (Dweck *et al.*, 1978). Taking this argument a stage further, it is possible that behaviour which in boys is seen as 'simple' naughtiness, capable of control by minor sanctions, may be regarded as evidence of emotional instability in girls.

The point about all these differences is that they are socially created. There is no obvious biological justification for any of them. They have developed in a social context and are maintained socially. Communities differ in the social roles they expect boys and girls, or men and women, to fill. Fundamentalist Christian groups have something in common with fundamentalist Islamic groups in differentiating sharply between the roles of men and women in the family and in society. Consequently they place a high priority on separate schools for boys and girls as a way of socialising them into the sex roles they see as desirable. Other Christian and Islamic groups have different views about the respective responsibilities of men and women in the family and in society, and consequently see the school's task differently.

All this raises a difficult question for teachers in state schools, even if their school is 'controlled' or 'aided' by a religious group. Both teachers and parents will have their own ideas about what sort of behaviour is 'appropriate' for boys and girls. Similarly, they will have ideas about the sort of knowledge and the sort of skills that are important for each sex. They are unlikely, however, to have selected a school either because of their own commitment to a particular view about girls' and boys' education or because of the school's stated policy. Thus, although they will have their own biases, expectations and prejudices, these may be implicit rather than explicit.

Ethnicity

Not all schools have a multi-ethnic pupil intake but all work in a multi-ethnic and multi-cultural society. In the 1960s and 1970s a long, acrimonious and largely futile debate raged over two questions whose educational implications were at best uncertain. The first was whether intelligence was inherited. The second assumed an affirmative answer and considered whether ethnic groups varied in their inherited intelligence. The principal interest in this debate for present purposes lies in what it tells us about psychologists. While many psychologists would like to claim that psychology is the impartial, scientific study of behaviour, the fact remains that they choose both the subjects of study and the methods. To believe that they set out in a disinterested way to discover whether intelligence is or is not inherited is naive. Much more frequently they set out to obtain evidence in support of a particular point of view. This led Sir Cyril Burt, the father of educational psychology in Britain, to publish articles using fraudulent data (Hearnshaw, 1979). Nor is it often legitimate to claim that psychologists have no control over how politicians or educationalists use the scientific evidence they obtain (Kamin, 1974). If you believe that one group of people is genetically superior in intelligence to another, whether the latter group be black, Irish or working class, it is a very short step to supporting a system that offers superior opportunities to the 'superior' group. The logical result is apartheid.[6]

In Britain numerous studies have been carried out into the measured intelligence (IQ) and educational attainments of children from different ethnic groups. Superficially, the majority of studies showed Afro-Caribbean children to be performing at a lower level than white children or Asian children, though there was substantial variation between different groups from Asia. More detailed analysis showed significant relationships between social class, family circumstances and length of time in Britain. When these were taken into account the differences in educational attainment became much smaller. A recent study has shown that Afro-Caribbean students in London secondary schools ended up with higher formal qualification than their white counterparts (Smith and Tomlinson, 1989). This study also demonstrated the influence of the school which the pupils attended on their examination results.

We said earlier that the debate over the inheritance of intelligence was long, acrimonious and largely futile. The futility lay partly in the concept of intelligence and partly in the confusion over the moral uses of the research. What counts as intelligence depends on the culture under investigation. Inevitably, researchers have to adopt a definition consistent with the views of the dominant culture in their society. This leads to the well-known conclusion that intelligence is what intelligence tests measure. As important, it is never possible to be certain that we have adequately taken account of all the variables that may affect a pupil's measured intelligence. The head of a residential special school for delicate children once claimed to David Galloway that earlier in his career he had demonstrated with the use of controls that pupils' IQ could be raised several points by thawing them out on the hot water pipes a few minutes before testing. Disentangling the complex web of school, family and environmental influences on test performance is infinitely more difficult. Yet these are essentially technical problems. Whether it is worth trying to overcome depends not on their technical difficulty but on the ethical purposes of the research.

In the 1960s and 1970s many ethnic minority groups opposed research programmes which compared their children's performance with that of the white majority. The reason was that they mistrusted the uses to which the white majority would put the research. In other words, they feared that the research would be used to justify their children's low achievements, if not to legitimise discrimination against them. In the 1980s many ethnic minority groups have insisted on monitoring their children's progress, seeing the results as a way of demonstrating inequality of opportunity and demanding better resources. Hence, research can never be separated from its perceived moral objectives.[7]

The school's role in creating equal opportunities

The rhetoric of the late 1980s demands equal opportunities for boys and girls. Some religious groups insist that boys and girls should not have the *same* opportunities since their responsibilities in later life will be *different*. They tend also to insist that provision of *different* opportunities does not mean that they have unequal value. The counter to this is that provision of different opportunities leads almost inevitably to inequality, with girls' education perceived as less important than boys'.

The school's role in a multi-ethnic society raises similar questions. The principle of equality of opportunity is not contentious but its implementation most certainly is. One view holds that schools should celebrate cultural diversity, arguing both that cultural traditions are interdependent and hence that children should learn about each other's cultures, and also that personal identity is strengthened by strong cultural ties. This view holds that schools should recognise and help to maintain children's home languages by appointing teachers who speak them, and in secondary schools offering them as an alternative to European languages for GCSE and 'A' level. This view would also seek to question the high status of 'public' activities, for example in the employment field, compared with 'private' activities predominantly performed by women, such as looking after young children. An alternative view is that schools should see their task principally in terms of education about British culture. Thus, the daily act of worship should generally be Christian in nature and the curriculum should be designed to teach all children about British cultural traditions and history. This essentially assimilationist philosophy is evident in the National Curriculum introduced by the 1988 Education Reform Act. This Act was, of course, a political measure. It contrasts in an interesting way with the dominant professional ideology which still insists on the importance of preparing trainee teachers for work in a multi-ethnic society (DES, 1989a).

We should note a dissenting ethnic minority voice at this stage. The idea that schools should seek to strengthen cultural identity has not gone unchallenged. There are two related arguments. First, the methods that schools use to support cultural identities constitute a thinly veiled attempt to legitimise discrimination. Secondly, parents feel that they can look after their children's cultural development and want schools to help them gain the knowledge and skills that will help them in the labour market. Thus Stone's (1981) research indicates that Afro-Caribbean parents were sceptical about the encouragement their children's teachers gave to their contribution to the school's sporting or musical reputation. What parents wanted was 'O' levels. Similarly Nash (1983) drew attention to the practice in New Zealand schools of encouraging clubs to promote awareness of Maori heritage while streaming Maori pupils into low status classes. The clubs, like brass bands and sports teams, could be seen as a way of socialising Maori pupils into accepting inferior status in the schools, and ultimately in society.

All this is somewhat remote from the more obvious evidence of sexism and racism in schools. It is now some years since the publishers of the Ladybird books dressed Jane in jeans, but sex role stereotyping is still evident in many of the most frequently used books in infant schools. In its most extreme form girls help mother with the housework while boys help father dig the garden or wash the car. Only a little more subtly, problems in mathematics books draw disproportionately on male characters. History presents a white, male, British version of events with emphasis on war. Children are taught about the Indian mutiny, not the first war of Indian independence. The geography and religious education syllabus, too, can encourage an ethnocentric perspective, seeing other countries and other religions from an anglocentric perspective. The curriculum, then, can all too easily become the mode through which the beliefs, values and prejudices of the dominant culture are transmitted.

This can be seen as 'institutionalised' sexism and racism. It is institutionalised in the sense that it arises from the unconscious assimilation of attitudes as a result of teachers' own socialisation, not from a conscious intent to discriminate against any particular group. Research by psychologists can help teachers to become more aware of their own attitudes and of the effect their classroom behaviour has on children's self-esteem or motivation. Research by psychologists can also provide evidence which is interpreted as legitimising existing attitudes and behaviour. Psychology, then, *can* be an instrument of social control. However, it can also be an instrument of change, helping teachers to explore ways of understanding their pupils and evaluating their own work as teachers. The same, of course, applies to sociology, philosophy and the study of history.

Individual or group differences?

Differences in gender, social class and ethnicity all refer to membership of identified groups. The relevance of this for teachers claiming to meet individual needs is that a sense of personal, or individual, identity, arises in a social context. By the time they start school, children's gender identity is well established, but how their concept of gender develops will be affected by their socialisation at school as well as at home. A school's equal opportunities policy may be reflected in the curriculum and in the relationships between teachers and children, and also in the relationship between teachers. In this case children may learn that responsibility is awarded according to ability rather than gender and that gender has little relevance to their educational progress through the curriculum. Alternatively the hidden messages conveyed through the curriculum and through interpersonal relationships in the school may be that decision making is a male preserve, at least in important matters, and that day-to-day activities are determined by gender rather than interest or ability.

To feel secure children, and adults, need to feel that they are members of a group. This was a recurring theme in the work of Emile Durkheim (1858–1917), one of the 'fathers' of educational sociology (e.g. Durkheim, 1933). Over 90 years ago Durkheim was writing about the importance of a sense of social cohesiveness, or solidarity. More recently Hargreaves (1982) argued that the 'cult of individualism' that pervades the British school system consistently underestimates the importance of a sense of group solidarity. Hargreaves was writing about secondary schools. He argued that when pupils feel they have little chance of achieving success in the school's official activities, they protect their self-esteem by identifying with other similarly disaffected pupils, and develop a group identity which depends on rejection of the school's aims and values.

Primary children seldom form themselves into the disaffected subgroups that appear in the final year of compulsory secondary education. A similar process is nevertheless evident even in infant and junior schools. It is seen when children obtain social recognition from other children, as well, incidentally, as their teacher's attention, for deliberately noisy behaviour or for failing to follow instructions. It is seen in the junior school boy whose sense of personal identity is maintained by his social reputation as clown of the class. It is seen in the girl whose reputation for absent-mindedness has become a standard joke in her class, as well as in her family.

We cannot, then, hope to understand individual differences simply by studying individual pupils. Children's behaviour and achievements have to be seen in a social context. Consequently we need to ask whether this context reduces the educational impact of differences between children or serves to increase them.

Conclusions: similarities or differences?

How far, then, does psychology help teachers to understand the differences between children? It is easy to give examples or research with obvious implications for teachers. Cross-cultural research, for example, illustrates the importance of differences in conventions about verbal and non-verbal behaviour. A classic example is eye contact. In many cultures, including the majority culture in Britain, a child's failure to make eye contact when talking to an authority figure is seen as 'shiftiness' or even insolence. In other cultures it would be insolent for a child to make eye contact with an elder, especially in a disciplinary situation. Teachers should clearly recognise situations in which verbal or non-verbal behaviour is likely to be misinterpreted.[8]

Yet examples of psychological research with immediate applications for teachers avoid a more important and more general question about differences between children. The central problem is best illustrated in the work on the inheritance of intelligence and in the development of normative tests. Briefly, the ideology of the person doing the research, or using the tests is likely to influence the uses to which the results are put. As the study of behaviour, psychology is value free, yet the mere fact of studying behaviour tells us nothing about the researcher's motivation and methods, nor about the uses to which he or she hopes to put the results. Thus the ideas of psychologists are not value free. Psychology offers a variety of methodologies for investigating educational problems. The problem may be how to teach *all* pupils more effectively, though in this case the researcher would have to make a moral and political judgement as to what counts as 'effective' education. Alternatively the problem may be how to identify 10–20 per cent of pupils for a privileged education leading to lucrative high-status jobs, as when children were separated at the age of 11 for a grammar school place. Psychology can help to create equality of opportunity, or to discriminate against particular groups.

Traditionally, educational psychology in Britain has been concerned with what distinguishes one pupil from another rather than with what they have in common. Indeed, differences could be described as the raison d'être of applied educational psychologists. The perceived ability of educational psychologists to identify the sources of individual differences and to discuss the educational implications constitutes a large part of their professional identity. Nevertheless, it is highly problematic. If provision of equal opportunities means anything it presumably means that factors such as social class, gender and race are not the basis for offering pupils qualitatively different experiences in school.

The problem with this view is that pupils are manifestly not all the same. Some have exceptional difficulty with all or parts of the curriculum. Others have, or present, behavioural problems. A legitimate argument is that children naturally need to learn what they have in common with their peers, but this learning can only take place if the educationally significant differences between them are recognised. The curriculum, then, must differentiate between children's different needs. This 'liberal' perspective provides an obvious role for educational psychologists in helping teachers to recognise and meet individual needs. An alternative perspective sees learning and behaviour difficulties as threatening teachers' need for control and hence their self-esteem. Here the educational psychologist's role could still lie in helping teachers to recognise and meet individual needs, but it could also be seen in terms of social control, with the emphasis on identifying problem children in order to remove them from the classroom or, at least, to suggest ways of reducing the difficulties they present. Either perspective leads to a consideration of special educational needs.

Notes and further reading

1. The most significant contributions to understanding the status of different forms of knowledge have been made by educational sociologists, for example: Bourdieu, P. (1977), Cultural Reproduction and Social Reproduction. In Karabel, J. and Halsey, A.K. (eds) *Power and Ideology in Education*. New York, Oxford University Press.

2. There is an extensive literature on the relationship between social disadvantage and educational progress. Two books provide particularly useful reviews:
   Rutter, M. and Madge, N. (1976) *Cycles of Disadvantage*. London, Heinemann.
   Mortimore, J. and Blackstone, T. (1982) *Disadvantage and Education*. London, Heinemann.

3. For reviews of research on school effectiveness, see:
   Purkey, M.C. and Smith, M.S. (1983) Effective Schools: A Review. *Elementary School Journal*, 8, 427–52.

4. The study of Junior Schooling in Inner London by Mortimore *et al.* (1988) should be read by all teachers. Critical reviews by N. Bennett and J. Winkley can be found in the *Times Educational Supplement*, 25 March 1988, p. 25.

5. For further examples of gender differentiation in the primary classroom see:
   French, J. and French, P. (1984) Gender Imbalances in the Primary Classroom: an interactional account. *Educational Research*, 26, 127–36.
   Whyte, J.C. (1983) *Beyond the Wendy House: sex role stereotyping in primary schools*. London, Schools Council.

6. Supporters of Piaget's concept of intelligence seek to overcome this problem. Piaget saw intelligent behaviour as successful adaptation to the environment. See: Piaget, J. (1936) *The Origin of Intelligence in the Child* (trans. M Cook, 1977). Harmondsworth, Penguin.

7. For useful reviews of research see:
Tomlinson, S. (1980) The educational performance of ethnic minority children. *New Community*, 8, 213–34
Smith. D.J. and Tomlinson, S. (1989) *The School Effect: a study of multi-racial comprehensives*. London, Policy Studies Institute.
8. For a review of cross-cultural differences in non-verbal communication see: Vogelaar, L.M.E. and Silverman, M.S. (1984) Non-verbal Communication in Cross-cultural Counselling: a literature review. *International Journal for the Advancement of Counselling*, 7, 41–57.
A fascinating study from New Zealand is provided by:
Metge, J. and Kinloch, P. (1978) *Talking Past Each Other: Problems of Cross Cultural Communication*. Wellington, New Zealand, Victoria University of Wellington.

Seminar suggestions

1. List the ways in which boys and girls are treated differently in the course of a typical day at the school you know best. Does this different treatment matter? What do children learn from it?
2. As you enter the classroom you hear one child calling another a 'black sod'. What do you do?
3. In Mortimore *et al.* (1988) *'School Matters: The Junior Years'*, read chapter 12, 'Towards More Effective Schooling'. This provides more explanation and detail for the twelve 'key factors' in effective schooling that are summarised in Table 2.1. Evaluate each of these factors in the light of your own experience. From *your* experience, either as a teacher or as a pupil, what do *you* see as key factors in effective schooling?
4. In what ways do you think schools can best mitigate the effects of social disadvantage?

CHAPTER 3

Special educational needs

Introduction

Which children are we talking about?

As Secretary of State for Education and Science, Margaret Thatcher in 1974 appointed Mary Warnock to chair a committee:

to review educational provision in England, Scotland and Wales for children and young people handicapped by disabilities of body or mind, taking account of the medical aspects of their needs, together with arrangements to prepare them for entering into employment; to consider the most effective use of resources; and to make recommendations.

The Committee published its report four years later (DES, 1978a). At this time roughly 2 per cent of children nationally were being educated in special schools or special classes. Other children with learning difficulties were taught in the 'remedial' departments of mainstream secondary schools or, in primary schools, by remedial teachers who were often employed part-time. Almost all such help was based on removing the child from the mainstream classroom. Special schools catered for the eleven categories of handicap recognised under the 1944 Education Act in the mistaken belief that a category of medical handicap could define the nature of a child's educational needs; some children in wheelchairs are able to benefit from the full range of the National Curriculum without special *educational* help, whereas children with a relatively minor but permanent injury to their writing hand may require specialised resources, at least in the short to medium term.

The Warnock Report recommended abolition of the categories recognised under the 1944 Act, replacing them with the generic concept of special educational needs. This referred to children with learning difficulties that might be mild, moderate or severe. It was expected that schools would normally be able to cater for children with mild learning difficulties without additional resources, whereas children with moderate amd severe learning difficulties would normally require multi-disciplinary assessment to identify their needs and determine the additional help required to meet them.

Perhaps the most well-known of Warnock's conclusions was that up to 15 per cent of children would require some form of special educational help at any one time, and up to 20 per cent at some stage of their school careers. Special educational needs, therefore, were seen as a responsibility for *all* teachers. In the same year, HMI in Scotland published an influential report arguing that at least 50 per cent of children could be said to have learning difficulties, and that mainstream schools should accept responsibility for them (Scottish Education Department, 1978).

The research on which the Warnock Committee based its conclusions was carried out by psychologists, child psychiatrists and community health specialists (e.g. Rutter *et al.*, 1975; Davie *et al.*, 1972). It described the prevalence of learning and behavioural difficulties among children of different ages. Yet while claiming to be based on solid research evidence, Warnock's conclusion was a political compromise based on a moral judgement. The research was based largely on children's results in intelligence and reading tests and on behaviour rating scales completed by parents and teachers. Intelligence and reading tests are designed to distinguish between children of differing ability. The behaviour rating scales contained items that were familiar to teachers, on the reasonable grounds that the research was investigating problems of immediate relevance to teachers. The design of the instruments ensured that a large minority of children could be identified as having, or presenting, problems. Any committee could use the results to identify an entirely arbitrary proportion of children as having special needs – 5, 10, 20, 30 or 50 per cent – and claim respectable research evidence in support of their conclusion. To have identified only 5 per cent of children as having special needs would have left the committee open to the charge that they simply had not recognised the range and complexity of problems facing teachers in mainstream schools. To have identified 50 per cent, like HMI in Scotland, would have invited ridicule from the government as unrealistic. Twenty per cent was a convenient political compromise. It was also a moral judgement, implying that teachers *ought* to be able to cater for roughly 80 per cent of their pupils without extra help, but that the most problematic 20 per cent *ought* to receive particular attention.

What do children with special educational needs have in common?

Among children with physical and sensory impairment, and children with severe intellectual handicap, there is a relatively even social class distribution. In other words children with these difficulties are about as likely to have professional as working-class parents. In the case of children with emotional and behavioural difficulties this is not the case. They are much more likely to come from manual working-class families. The same applies to children with mild learning difficulties in mainstream schools and to children with moderate learning difficulties, who could be regarded as having a moderate level of intellectual impairment, in special schools.

Children with mild and moderate learning difficulties and/or emotional and behavioural difficulties constitute a majority of the 20 per cent Warnock regarded as having special educational needs. As well as coming predominantly from manual working-class homes, these children contain a disproportionate number of boys – between two and three boys for every girl and also a disproportionate number of children from ethnic minority groups. The common element in learning and behavioural difficulties is that teachers find the children's progress and/or behaviour disturbing. The social class, ethnic and gender bias suggest that identification of special needs may be based as much on the teacher's need for stability in the classroom as on the child's need for special help. This suggestion is supported by consistent evidence that children's educational progress is no better at special schools than at mainstream schools (e.g. Carlberg and Kavale, 1980; Galloway and Goodwin, 1987). Hence, provision for special educational needs raises ethical issues as well as practical ones of school and classroom organisation.[1]

Ethical issues

We cannot need something without in some sense also wanting it (see pp. 5–9). Learning and behavioural problems at school are usually identified by teachers. In identifying a child as having special educational needs teachers may be drawing attention to their concern about:

1.   the child him or herself;
2.   the effect the child is having on the progress or the behaviour of other children in the class;
3.   the inadequacy of the resources available within the classroom;
4.   the effect of the child's presence on their own job satisfaction and sense of personal well-being.

None of these, of course are exclusive of the others. They do nevertheless illustrate two crucial points. First, we cannot usefully think about children with special needs in isolation from the school and classroom context in which these needs are apparent. Secondly, the needs of children and the needs of teachers are inter-related. Attempting to focus on the child's needs alone, for example by means of individual intelligence or personality assessment, individualises the problem by pretending that other factors, such as social interaction within the classroom, the teacher's experience and ability or the availability of appropriate resources are irrelevant. Bluntly, it makes the child responsible for any short-comings that may lie within the school or classroom.

Equal opportunities

The Warnock Report was adamant that special educational needs was a relative concept, not an absolute one. Whether or not a child was considered to have special needs would depend on the circumstances, not simply on any supposedly scientific measure of personality or intelligence. It is doubtful, however, whether the committee fully recognised the implications of its own position. The report emphasises the differences between children with special needs and other children, and never gets to grips with ways in which schools might contribute to pupils' difficulties. Nor did the report ever get to grips with the moral question of pupils' entitlement to participate in activities available to other children. These issues were identified a great deal more clearly in the report of a committee chaired by John Fish, a former HMI, for the Inner London Education Authority (ILEA, 1985). This committee was clear that:

The aims of education for children and young people with disabilities and significant handicaps were the same as those for all children and young people. They should have opportunities to achieve these aims and to associate with their contemporaries, whether similarly disabled or not, and have access to the whole range of opportunities in education, training, leisure and community activities available to all. Disabilities and significant difficulties do not diminish the right to equal access to, and participation in, society (para. 1.1.22).

This insistence on equal opportunities for pupils with special needs contained both a moral and a political statement. The former is self-evident. The latter reflected the concern of elected members on the Inner London Education Committee that the school system was currently offering unequal, and implicitly inferior opportunities to working-class children and to members of ethnic minority groups. Gender was also a concern of the committee, and the overrepresentation of boys in schools for children with learning and behavioural difficulties was relevant here. Taking the argument a step further the report maintained that:

children and young people may have the handicapping effects of their disabilities increased by social factors and educational experiences (para. 1.1.36)

From here it was a short step to the conclusion that:

Meeting special educational needs is an integral aspect of education for all (para. 1.1.45).

Responses to special educational needs

A deficit model

Advice from psychologists, notably Sir Cyril Burt, had been influential in the decision in the 1944 Education Act to adopt a tripartite system of grammar, technical and secondary modern schools. However, the Act assumed that some children would not fit into this system. These children would have to be identified and 'special' education provided for them. Psychologists who claimed a 'scientific' basis for selecting children for grammar schools could make a similar claim in selecting children for special schools. Under the Act school medical officers were able to 'ascertain' a child as suffering from one of ten handicapping conditions. As there were insufficient educational psychologists to carry out the necessary assessments, doctors were trained to administer intelligence tests, and these formed the basis for ascertainment as 'educationally subnormal'. As educational psychologists gradually became more numerous, they claimed expertise in identifying educational needs, arguing that doctors should stick to the implications for teachers of any relevant medical conditions. This trend culminated in the 1981 Education Act which imposed on all LEAs an obligation to obtain an educational psychologist's report, together with reports from teachers and school medical officers, as part of a multi-disciplinary assessment of a child's special educational needs.

The emphasis, though, remained on identifying the special needs of individual pupils and on production of a 'statement' setting out how the LEA intended to meet these needs. The 1981 Act is responsible for the dreadful neologism 'statemented children' becoming educational jargon in Britain.[2] The model, then, remained a deficit one. In practice, if not necessarily in theory, the problem was still seen as finding remedies for the deficits, or difficulties of individual children. Psychological tests had always claimed to identify current functioning. Their claims to predict future performance had been made with considerable confidence until research showed that children's IQ could change substantially within 2–3 years (e.g. Hindley and Owen, 1978). Teachers, administrators and many educational psychologists nevertheless continued to rely on them.

Yet the deficit model with its primary emphasis on fitting the child into the system, as opposed to analysing the system to see why it was failing to meet the child's needs, was inappropriate both in theory and in practice. The practical problem was that if as many as 20 per cent of children had special needs, let alone the 50 per cent identified by HMI (Scottish Educational Department, 1978) in Scotland, then responses must be institutional rather than individual. With classes of up to 30, and in some LEAs 35, teachers have limited time to design individual programmes for children, let alone put them into practice. The aim, therefore, must be *to help individuals through class or group activities.* The theoretical problem is that children's personal and educational development takes place, for better or worse, in social contexts. Hence, if we are serious about enhancing opportunities for personal and educational development, we must have regard to the quality of the child's experience as a member of a class. Observation of children, whether they have special needs or not, shows that they can learn from each other. Indeed the quality of learning experiences depends to a considerable extent on how far a teacher organises activities to make this possible. Attempts to select individual children for extra help in withdrawal groups simply ignores these problems.

Support for learning within a whole school approach to special educational needs

The argument presented so far implies that schools will not cater effectively for pupils with special needs on a piecemeal basis in which special provision is bolted on to what is provided for the majority of pupils. Rather, provision for the majority has to be sufficiently flexible to accommodate pupils with special needs. This is the essential feature of a whole school approach. It acknowledges the possibility that the school's organisation, curriculum, teaching methods and provision for pupil welfare may be contributing to pupil's difficulties rather than meeting them. Simmons (1986) identified three characteristics of a whole school approach. It should ensure:

(a) that *all* teachers, not just those primarily concerned with special needs, should be aware of the ranges of needs that might arise in their classrooms;
(b) that *all* teachers should be responsible for assessing the difficulties of material used in their lessons; and
(c) that *all* teachers should have access to specialised help in dealing, inside the classroom, with children with learning difficulties (p. 19).

It is worth noting that the DES (1988b) seems to share this view. In a circular letter to all higher education institutions involved in INSET provision, the DES asserted that training for teachers with designated responsibility for meeting special needs in ordinary schools should help them in:

identifying impediments to pupils' learning and devising strategies to overcome them;

considering the implications, for the curriculum and full life of the school as a whole, of the presence of children with a range of special educational needs;

implementing appropriate forms of organisation for the additional and supplementary help which will give such children access to the full range of the curriculum (p. 5).

Our only reservation about Simmons' and the DES' criteria is that the changing approach to special educational needs requires explicit attention to the rights and responsibilities of pupils as well as to what is expected of teachers. In particular three issues have recurred when we have explored the concept of special educational needs on INSET courses:

1. that *all* pupils should have access to the full range of the curriculum;
2. that *all* pupils should have the opportunity, be expected and be seen to contribute usefully to the life and work of the school;
3. that *all* pupils, irrespective of ability, should be encouraged and expected to develop an awareness of, and respect for, individual differences.

The first of these requires further comment. The National Curriculum has to be accessible to all pupils, unless a statement of their special needs exempts them from part or all of its requirements. In addition, head teachers can exempt pupils on a temporary basis in certain quite strictly specified circumstances (see DES, 1989b). Yet the fact that children with severe or complex difficulties cannot reasonably be expected to meet the attainment targets for their age-group does not mean that the whole curriculum area is inappropriate. The 1988 Education Reform Act insisted not only that the National Curriculum applies to the large majority of pupils with special needs, but also that exemption can only be granted in restricted circumstances, and then only if alternative curricular arrangements are stated. This may have done more to stimulate constructive thought about the curriculum for pupils with special needs than the Warnock Report and the 1981 Education Act put together.[3]

Models of support

Until the late 1980s, the most frequent form of support for children with special needs in primary schools was to remove them from the classroom for extra help with reading or, less frequently, mathematics. Often the teachers concerned were appointed to a school on a part-time basis, or less frequently relieved from full-time responsibility for a class to withdraw selected children for special help. This model still exists in many schools, and is maintained in some LEAs by peripatetic reading and language services which see their task as working with individuals or small groups. A good deal of research has been carried out on the effectiveness of this kind of 'remedial' teaching (e.g. Sampson, 1975; Tobin and Pumfrey, 1976). The evidence suggests that children tend to make quite good progress while attending remedial groups, but that this progress is unlikely to be maintained when they return full-time to their regular classes.

On theoretical grounds this is only to be expected. Social learning theory emphasises the importance of context in people's behaviour.[4] Skills that children learn in one context will not necessarily transfer to another unless they are consciously practised in the new context. This indicates the most common problem with withdrawal groups. There is seldom time for meetings that might enable withdrawal group teachers to base their activities on work which the rest of the class would be doing. Consequently the remedial work often bears little relationship to the children's regular classroom experience. This means: (a) that they receive no direct help with the activities they find difficult; (b) that on return to the classroom they have little opportunity to consolidate the skills they have learned in the remedial group, since the rest of the class is following entirely different activities; (c) that class teachers receive little or no practical guidance on how they might be able to help children with learning difficulties, since responsibility lies with the remedial specialist.

A whole-school approach to special needs aims to overcome these problems by giving children, and class teachers, support within the ordinary classroom. The form this support takes can vary widely, depending on the needs both of the children and of their teachers. It can include:

1. planning units of work to enable *all* children to take part in an active way;
2. the special needs teacher working with an individual or with a group of children with learning difficulties;
3. the specialist teacher working temporarily with the majority of the class, releasing the class teacher to work with children with special needs;
4. planning assessment, monitoring and record keeping procedures;
5. planning and implementing programmes to tackle 'difficult' behaviour in individuals or groups;
6. assessing the readability level of materials in daily use in the classroom.

In theory, providing help within the ordinary class overcomes the problems of learning transfer that bedevilled remedial withdrawal groups, while at the same time developing the class teacher's own skills in recognising special needs and responding to them. In practice formidable problems still arise. Although many LEAs have asked all head teachers to identify a coordinator with responsibility for special needs provision, staffing constraints mean that few primary class teachers can expect a great deal of in-class support. Also, the relationship between class teachers and a specialist colleague working alongside them is unfortunately not always an easy one. The specialist's suggestions can be interpreted as criticism and her or his presence perceived as a threat to the class teacher's autonomy.[5]

Future trends in light of the 1988 Education Reform Act

Under the 1988 Act larger primary schools are included in LEA schemes for financial delegation to schools. This means that the governors have a responsibility for staffing, subject to their annual budget. In most LEA's, part of the annual allocation is intended for special needs, but it does not follow that it will actually be used in this way. Also, resources for children with a statement of their special needs may be funded separately. This could lead some head teachers to refer an increasing number of children for formal assessment in order: (a) to obtain additional resources that the school could not otherwise afford; (b) to obtain the child's exemption from some or all of the requirements of the National Curriculum.

Whether this happens will depend largely on the clarity and consistency of LEA policies on statementing. It is worth repeating, though, that the 1988 Act may have done more to stimulate discussion about the curriculum for children with special needs than the 1981 Act. The National Curriculum can only be dis-applied in highly specific circumstances (DES, 1989b). Moreover, schools will be judged by their pupils' performance in the national testing programmes at ages 7, 11, 14 and 16. It follows that schools will have to give serious thought to the effectiveness of their provision for the less able 20, 40 or 50 per cent of their pupils. Schools which concentrate on a small élite of pupils, as in the days of the 11+, may find it difficult to conceal from parents the inadequacy of provision for academically less able children.

The fact that all children will be following the National Curriculum is likely to discourage a return to the remedial withdrawal groups of the 1960s and 1970s. Rather, the emphasis is likely to be on finding ways to make the curriculum more readily accessible to children with learning difficulties. Primary teachers have long prided themselves on having full-time responsibility for their classes, but have not always recognised the importance of specialist advice if they are to teach all children and all curriculum areas effectively. HMI (1978) referred caustically to as many as 25 per cent of teachers with posts of special responsibility having an influence that extended beyond their own classroom – implying, of course, that 75 per cent did not. Today *all* teachers are expected to develop the expertise to provide leadership in a specified curriculum area. This has interesting implications for teachers with responsibility for special needs.

Currently many special needs coordinators in primary schools work directly with class teacher colleagues in providing support for children with special needs. The limitation here is that the special needs coordinator may have no specific expertise in, say, science, yet has to help a colleague find ways to make the science syllabus interesting and enjoyable for children with a range of learning and behavioural difficulties. The special needs coordinator should have expertise in developing materials suitable for children with special needs, but will not necessarily have particular expertise in the area with which the child, or class teacher, is having problems. It follows that special needs coordinators may find they can use their expertise more effectively by working with the designated teacher for each curriculum area rather than with class teachers. The science specialist for example, would then be able to help colleagues adapt their class programme in the light of the children's needs. Subject specialists, therefore, would have responsibility for the full range of needs within their own curriculum area, with the special needs coordinator acting as a consultant when difficulties arose.

Children with more complex or severe difficulties

We are referring here to children with difficulties who call for additional resources to those routinely available in mainstream schools. These can take many forms including severe intellectual handicap, physical impairment, visual or auditory impairment or speech and communication difficulties. Children with moderate levels of intellectual handicap and children with severe emotional and behavioural difficulties can also present substantial learning and management problems in ordinary classes, calling for some kind of additional support. Under the 1944 Act children with these more complex or severe difficulties were 'ascertained' as suffering from a category of handicap and the LEA was obliged to place them in a special school or class catering for the category in question. Educational psychologists and school medical officers cooperated, and sometimes competed, in identifying children for the available facilities.

This raises some interesting questions about the role of educational psychologists and about the use to which educational psychology is put. Superficially the expansion of special schools following the 1944 Act could be seen as a logical extension to the tripartite system of grammar, technical and secondary modern schools. However, it can also be seen as a logical extension to the institutions for mentally handicapped people that had proliferated in the Victorian and post-Victorian era.

Special schools and institutional provision for handicapped adults can be seen in two lights. A conventional view sees such provision as a benevolently humanitarian attempt to cater for people needing specialised forms of care, treatment or teaching. A more cynical view sees them as an attempt to remove from circulation people whose presence poses a threat to the stability of society. Members of the eugenics movement advocated life-long segregation of the mentally retarded on the grounds that their mental, and associated moral degeneracy would create unmanageable problems in and for society. Influential books in the nineteenth century traced the descendants of problem families and claimed high rates of delinquency and sexual promiscuity to be associated with mental deficiency (e.g. Dugdale, 1977). More recently David Galloway remembers an eminent lecturer on his psychology degree course in the late 1960s expressing concern about the fertility of working-class families. Because they bred more rapidly than the middle class, and tended to have a lower IQ, the average intelligence of the nation was likely to fall.[6]

The political nature of this view has been dealt with elsewhere (see Kamin, 1974 and Chapter 8). Its scientific underpinning has also been discredited, not least with the exposure as fraudulent of much of Burt's work on the inheritance of intelligence (Hearnshaw, 1979). It is no longer supported in the crude form proposed by the eugenicists, at least openly. Nevertheless, there is still an interesting parallel in school and LEA responses to special educational needs.

Children with learning or behavioural difficulties pose a threat not only to the stability of the classroom, but also to their teacher's self-esteem. In a literal sense they are *disturbing* to teach. This is confirmed by research on stress in teaching which consistently shows teachers reporting learning and behavioural problems as a major source of stress from day-to-day teaching (e.g. Dunham, 1984). The 1988 Education Reform Act introduced national testing programmes with the possibility that publication of the results would lead to highly publicised comparisons between schools. In this context pressure to remove 'misfits' from the mainstream could grow. Although the Warnock Report (DES, 1981) and the 1981 Education Act are widely believed to have encouraged the integration of children with special needs into mainstream schools, the evidence that this is actually happening is far from clear. Swann's (1985) analyses of DES statistics showed an increase in the number of children with sensory impairment in mainstream schools. This was not, however, the case with learning difficulties of a 'moderate' nature. For these children, and to a slightly lesser extent for children with emotional and behavioural difficulties the trend was in the opposite direction, towards increased segregation from the mainstream.

The obvious question is whether this should be a matter for concern. Special schools are designed to meet special needs, so surely they must provide more appropriate teaching? There are two ways of dealing with this question. First, research has quite consistently shown that children tend to make better educational progress in mainstream schools. Several literature reviews have failed to find a single study showing children with moderate learning difficulties making better educational progress in special schools (e.g. Galloway and Goodwin, 1987). Children with physical impairments too, appear able to make good educational progress in mainstream primary schools (e.g. E. Anderson, 1973), as do children with hearing impairment (e.g. Lynas, 1985).

The second response is perhaps less straightforward. By definition, special schools that operate in isolation from the mainstream cannot meet certain needs, for example:

1. the need to learn to play and work with 'non-handicapped' peers;
2. to develop an understanding of their own abilities *and* difficulties in the context of mainstream expectations;
3. to receive the 'broad and balanced' curriculum available to children in mainstream schools, including the extra-curricular activities;
4. to strengthen their sense of being valued members of the local community by attending the school which serves that community.

All these points are based on the value judgement that children with special needs 'ought' to attend their local school and that LEAs 'ought' to provide them, and their teachers, with the resources necessary for this to be successful. Research evidence supports this value judgement but did not give rise to it.

Implications for the educational psychologists

Where does all this leave educational psychologists? Psychologists, too, live in and are part of, a social world. The idea that psychologists, or any other scientists, spend their time in the disinterested pursuit of truth is naive. Psychologists were active in the eugenics movement. They believed strongly in the moral justification of their views, and used their positions of influence in universities and on government committees to claim scientific status for their personal beliefs. Some of Cyril Burt's cursory assessments of parents' and indeed children's intelligence merely provide the best known and most notorious examples (Hearnshaw, 1979).

Once a special facility is established, whether it be a subnormality hospital or a special school, power is vested in the people who control admissions to it. In the nineteenth century doctors claimed expertise in identifying 'patients' for subnormality institutions. They retained this power until after the 1944 Education Act, but were increasingly challenged by the new and rapidly developing profession of educational psychologists.

Psychologists argued, (a) that they had greater expertise in the 'scientific' assessment of intelligence, and (b) that in any case, *educational* decisions could not sensibly be made on the basis of *medical* assessment. From 1975 LEAs were advised to consult educational psychologists before providing a special school place (DES, 1975). The 1981 Education Act required them to do so as part of the assessment leading to a formal statement of a child's special needs.

Yet all of this was predicated on the deficit model. In other words, assessment focused on what children could *not* do, and how they *differed* from other children. The Fish report emphasised that the aims of education for children with special needs were the same as for all children (ILEA, 1985). Hence, an equally legitimate focus would be on what they *could* do, and on what they had in common with other children. This does not mean that we ignore a child's difficulties and the resources needed to overcome or reduce them. It does, nevertheless, imply that assessment of special educational needs leads in a different direction. The deficit model is orientated towards separate provision, either in a special school or by means of a withdrawal group for extra help with, say, reading. In contrast the alternative model is oriented towards the 'normal' environment and the resources needed to enable this environment to cater adequately for the child.

Even this, however, can be criticised as having too narrow a focus on the individual child. Hargreaves (1982) has attacked the 'cult of individualism' which pervades education in Britain. Educational psychology has provided powerful support for this cult. The 1981 Education Act effectively created two categories of children with special needs, (a) those whose needs could be met within the school's existing resources; these children would not need a formal assessment leading to the 'protection' of a statement of their special needs, and (b) those whose needs could not be met without extra help, and who therefore *would* require a statement.

The problem here is that the need for extra help depends on the quality of resources currently available. Principal among these is the teacher him or herself. It follows that *children's* learning and behavioural difficulties may reveal their *teacher's* needs. The teacher may simply need additional resources, but the problem may also lie in teaching methods, classroom organisation, lesson preparation and the use of existing resources. In other words the needs of children and of teachers are interrelated.

All this can create substantial tensions for educational psychologists. Their only statutory responsibility is for assessment of special educational needs under the 1981 Education Act. In principle, the fact that they work in schools and with teachers enables them to see children's needs in the context of their school and classroom experience. In principle, then, educational psychologists are well placed to identify teacher's needs as well as children's needs, since in practice they are inextricably interrelated. Nevertheless, visiting psychologists have to exercise the greatest caution to avoid appearing to 'blame' a teacher for a child's difficulties. To appear to be criticising a teacher colleague is to run the charge of being regarded as insensitive, ill-informed, even 'unprofessional'. In consequence psychologists can often find themselves forced back on to a deficit model of special educational needs, seeing the problem as lying 'in' the child and/or the family.

Contrary, perhaps, to the intentions of legislation, the 1981 Education Act encouraged this tendency with its detailed requirements for formal assessment of special needs. These required LEAs to seek advice from teachers, an educational psychologist and a school doctor, and attempted to safeguard parents' interests by giving them numerous rights of consultation and of appeal against LEA decisions. Tutt (1985) has criticised the concept of special needs implied in the Act as inappropriate, inadequate and detrimental. It is, he claims, inappropriate to children's interests in its focus on the individual child, with a corresponding neglect of the possible limitations in the school or classroom context; it is inadequate as it provides no guidance on the range or scope of special needs, nor on how or where they should be met. It is detrimental to children's interests by extending almost indefinitely the 'net' of children covered by a formal control system.

The first of Tutt's objections has created pressures on educational psychologists in some LEAs to define children's needs in the light of available resources (Goacher *et al.*, 1988). The reason, of course, lies in reluctance to accept expensive commitments at a time of financial restraint. LEAs have also varied widely in their policy on carrying out formal assessments. Few LEAs resist requests from parents, but they vary widely in how far they encourage their own teacher and educational psychologist employees to refer children for assessment. Some LEAs provide a statement for twice as many children as others (Goacher *et al.*, 1988).

The minutiae of assessment procedures may have had an additional consequence. The House of Commons Education, Science and Arts Committee (1987) received evidence from HMI, that few LEAs had adopted a coherent policy for special educational needs, and even fewer had formulated a coherent plan for implementing the policy they had adopted. The implication here is that the Act may have encouraged LEAs to respond to special needs as they arose on an *ad hoc* basis, without giving serious thought to the rationale for their overall provision or to its coherence. This led to some odd situations in which LEAs had formally adopted policies of integration, but continued to allocate resources in a way that made integration difficult, if not impossible to achieve (see Galloway and Goodwin, 1987).

The 1981 Education Act has nevertheless had some beneficial consequences. It has undoubtedly raised teachers' general awareness of the range and scope of children's learning and behavioural difficulties. It is also leading to more active parental participation in children's assessment. Following from this, parents are becoming increasingly vocal and explicit in demanding the sort of provision they consider necessary. Often, though by no means invariably, this is in mainstream schools.

We are advocating a model which emphasises what children with special needs have in common with other children rather than their differences. This implies the importance for children with special needs and for other children of developing an appreciation of individual differences. In addition, the emphasis on the school and classroom context implicitly acknowledges the mutual adaptation that takes place between individuals and their social 'niche' (see Chapter 1). Recognising the scope and range of special educational needs and seeking to meet them in mainstream schools does not just have implications for the 2 per cent who had traditionally been taught in special schools, nor just for the 20, 40 or 50 per cent who were thought by Warnock, Sir Keith Joseph or HMI, to have special needs, to be under-achieving or to have learning difficulties. It also has implications for all other pupils *and* for their teachers.

Conclusions

Teachers often perceive children with learning and behavioural problems as a source of stress. These children illustrate the limits to teachers' competence and threaten the stability of the classroom. The children concerned are disproportionately boys, from working-class families and members of ethnic minority groups. The evidence that at least 20 per cent of pupils have special needs at some stage in their school career, or according to HMI in Scotland 50 per cent, raises huge questions about the nature of the school system and its success in catering for large minorities of children.

Finding effective ways to teach children with a wide variety of abilities and backgrounds is part of each teacher's professional development. Relationships with children and seeing children making progress have been identified as the principal sources of job satisfaction for primary teachers (e.g. Holdaway, 1978; Galloway *et al.*, 1985). Seen in this light, children with special needs provide unique opportunities for job satisfaction. The focus, though, will be on the quality of teaching for the class as a whole and on ways of meeting individual needs within the mainstream curriculum.

We can look at the similarities and differences between children in terms of their curricular entitlement and in terms of the teaching methods appropriate to their needs. The principles of metacognition and self-assessment apply as much in teaching children with special needs as in everything else teachers do in school. However, special needs impose particular pressures on teachers to recognise contextual influences on children's development. These naturally include the home environment. They also include the other children in the class, school and classroom organisation, the range and availability and use of resources, and teaching methods. In other words, effectiveness in identifying and catering for special needs is inextricably linked with the effectiveness in teaching the class as a whole. This, then, is an appropriate time to consider some recent work on classroom interaction.

Notes and further reading

1. The issues raised in this paragraph have been developed in work on the sociology and politics of special educational needs. See, for example:
   Barton L. and Tomlinson S. (eds) (1984) *Special Education and Social Interests.* London, Croom Helm.
   Barton L. (ed.) (1989) *Special Educational Needs: Myth or Reality?* Lewes, Falmer Press.
2. For further discussion of the 1981 Education Act see: Hegarty, S. (1987) *Meeting Special Needs in Ordinary Schools.* London, Cassell.
   Gipps, C., Cross, H. and Goldstein, H. (1987) *Warnock's Eighteen Per Cent: Children with special needs in primary schools.* Lewes, Falmer Press.
   Pearson L. and Lindsay, G. (1986) *Special Needs in the Primary School.* Windsor, NFER-Nelson.
3. Initial response to the 1988 Education Reform Act from special educators were almost uniformly hostile. For an alternative perspective, which argues that the Act could have beneficial effects, see: Galloway, D. (1990) Was the Gerbil a Marxist Mole? In P. Evans and V. Varma (eds) *Special Education: Past, Present and Future.* Lewes, Falmer Press.
4. For a discussion of social learning theory see:
   Bandura, A. (1974) Behaviour Theory and Models of Man. *American Psychologist*, 29, 859–69.
   Bower, G.K. and Hildegard E.R. (1981) *Theories of Learning.* Englewood Cliffs, New Jersey, Prentice-Hall.
5. Recent books on a whole-school approach to special educational needs are:
   Ainscow, M. and Florek, A. (eds) (1989) *Special Educational Needs: Towards a Whole-School Approach.* London, David Fulton.

Ramasut, A. (ed.) (1989) *Whole-School Approaches to Special Needs.* Lewes, Falmer Press.

6.   For a more detailed account of the 'social control' perspective on special education see: Tomlinson, S. (1982) *The Sociology of Special Education.* London, Routledge and Kegan Paul.

Seminar suggestions

1.   (a) Think of a child with special needs in the class you know best. Write 5–10 lines explaining why you regard this child as having special needs.

   (b) Now write a brief report – two or three paragraphs – indicating the things this child *can* do, and how your future teaching with this child could build on their capabilities.

   In pairs discuss the different 'pictures' of each child that emerge from these two exercises. How far does the first lead to the deficit model described in the text, and the second to a whole-school/class approach?

2.   Describe the organisation of provision for special educational needs in the school each group member knows best. What are its strengths and limitations?

3.   What methods do teachers in your school(s) use in assessing children's special educational needs? How far do these methods help teachers in planning future work with children? What alternatives are possible?

CHAPTER 4

Interaction in classrooms

Learning how to behave

Before they start school young children have become used to adults expecting them to behave in different ways depending on the context. In the park they may be encouraged to run around and make a noise, but not in the house. When they start school they again find that different tasks have their own expectations and requirements. Children usually learn very quickly how to conform to adult classroom expectations. For example, the way that most young children discriminate between what is allowed on the big blocks and not permitted at the painting easels is clear evidence of their ability to learn rapidly and efficiently, often with minimal explicit instruction from their teacher.

If we observe two 5 year-olds, Jenny and Paul, on their entry to reception class we can see subtle processes at work as they pick up cues and learn the complex rules of classroom life. Both children have had pre-school playgroup experience and Jenny with an older sister at school is keyed into some of the more obvious rituals of 'big school'. Autonomy is required of them as they find their coat pegs and deposit their belongings. Paul has to be told what to do, Jenny already knows. Both children stand for a while and gaze around the room. The teacher is engaged in conversation with parents, but with an eye on the children. She tells them to 'sit on the carpet' and wait for her. Jenny skips over, Paul does not move. Jenny knows that you do what the teacher asks. That is not yet clear to Paul. When the teacher joins the seated children Paul is still standing near the coat racks. He does not respond to the invitation 'come and join us Paul', despite the 'there's a good boy'. Neither is he enticed by 'there are a lot of interesting things to talk about this morning'. Still believing he does not have to follow an adult's instructions, he declines. Later that morning Jenny is busily at play in the home corner and Paul is jumping off the big blocks with a group of boys. He continues to jump noisily despite a change of activity to 'tidy up time'. The teacher clearly has a problem as Paul must not be seen 'to get away with it'. She takes Paul aside and explains about tidying up. He stops the noisy behaviour, but still refuses to join the group for morning drink and story.

The behaviour continues for a few days with Jenny increasing the range of her activities as she learns the house rules of water play, painting, book choosing, and so on. By remaining an outsider Paul is slower to learn and restricts his activities to the big blocks and the compulsory tasks set by the teacher. Interactions with his teacher continue to be invitational and encouraging. His induction into the rules of the classroom comes eventually through friendship with another block jumper whom he imitates and with whom he widens his repertoire of activities. He can at last be regarded to be initiated when seen grinning at the teacher while flouting the 'tidy up' rule.

The two 5 year-olds have had to learn to cope with a wide range of interactions not simply with adults and children, but in a variety of contexts. Noise is allowed at 'choosing time' but not at 'story time', look after your own property but tidy up for everyone, work on your own at the puzzle table, but join in for story and drink, water play must be sensible but you can fool around in the playground, when teachers issue 'invitations' you must not refuse. You can chat to your teacher when you are alone but not in a group. The list is endless. What is apparent to those adults who try to make sense of classroom life is that interaction occurs in contexts and that different contexts demand different styles of behaviour from children.

Classroom contexts

At first glance it would appear that the teacher as the creator of the contexts is very much in control of them. However, a closer look at selection of resources, planning of the classroom and choice of teaching styles reveals that teachers are, at least, guided by a variety of influences. Each school will have its curriculum priorities whether these are determined by government, school catchment area, locality, arbitrary decisions of the head or joint processes in staff meetings. These in turn are affected by the funding that represents national and local priorities. Resourcing is limited by finance and availability; is the E. J. Arnold catalogue the greatest influence on British Primary Education? Teaching styles and classroom organisation depend greatly on their acceptability to colleagues and Local Authority advisers. A hidden curriculum may be transmitted by the teacher but she or he is usually the agent of the value systems at work in the school if not the wider community. Teachers also respond to parental expectations if only to achieve a compromise. The learning contexts inhabited by pupils, then, appear to be constructed by teachers who represent prevailing cultural and political priorities.

These contexts require different behaviours. The classroom shop demands turn-taking, politeness, careful communication. The home corner provides a place for emotional fantasy play. The climbing frame calls for confidence, physical skill and a little risk-taking. Written work at the table demands listening skills, concentration and manual dexterity. Different noise levels and interaction with peers are allowed at each. Similarly the role of the teacher will differ from complete absence, to safety watchdog, to direct interaction, for example through writing the child's sentences or providing explanations.

Clearly contexts are important because they provide the opportunities for action for both child and teacher. Mathematical language occurs while the child is weighing, while listening skills are improved and information imparted in teacher-led sessions. A study by Anne Edwards (1988) reveals that even 4 year-olds in nursery schools can distinguish between contexts in which they feel good or bad about themselves and where certain behaviours are tolerated or not.

As interactions not only occur in contexts, but are to an extent determined by them it is important that any examination of classroom interactions take situations into account. This point is not only of relevance to understanding the notion of classroom interaction at a theoretical level, but also to the daily assessments that teachers make of children. If a child only exhibits time-wasting behaviour during mathematics tasks or immediately prior to 'home time' then further inquiry should start from there.

Becoming a pupil

At the more theoretical level what we are arguing is that 'being a pupil' is a 'niche' which is waiting to be occupied and into which the child enters. Shotter (1984) as seen in Chapter 1, has described childhood in much these terms. He talks of the opportunities for development available to children as the niche that their culture has created for them in order to turn them into the adults that culture desires. The experiences or opportunities for development available within primary school classrooms are constructed with the intention of shaping children into effective learners and manageable members of the learning group. When these intentions are not realised we need to look at the developmental opportunities as they exist within the niche as well as at the child.

It follows, then, that when we talk of interaction we cannot regard it as a one-way process. While the child is adapting to becoming a pupil elements of the classroom niche are also accommodating to the child's demands. Thus teachers may rearrange classroom furniture or use new techniques or resources to achieve their ends. The child as pupil is produced as a result of negotiations between the child as learner and the teacher who is the creator of a specific pupil niche. Children have to renegotiate with each adult as they move through the school. They soon become adept at this as usually expectations of their behaviour fall into a clear range and teacher cues are remarkably similar (French and Peskett, 1986).

Shotter (1984) described the aim of childhood as the creation of autonomous adults: while this may be true of many cultures, there may be more debate over whether it is the aim of schooling. Developmental psychologists (e.g. Newson 1974; Schaffer, 1977; Trevarthen, 1978) argue that children learn to become autonomous, free-standing members of society as a result of high quality interactions with their carers. High quality interactions involve the adult in 'turn-taking', mutual respect and tuning in to the world of the child. So important is mutuality, that in the very early stages the adult acts as if there is equality in the relationship even though the infant cannot yet participate and subsequently the child is encouraged to enter the dialogue as a full partner as soon as possible.

Can it be said that dialogues of this quality regularly occur in classrooms? Habermas (1972) talks of true communication as best achieved between equal partners in a dialogue. The world of the school and demands made on teachers would seem to make this unlikely. It is difficult to find examples in everyday adult life which might illustrate the sense of powerlessness experienced by young children in classrooms. Habermas himself probably comes nearest as his own concerns stemmed from his observations of inequality in the client–psychotherapist relationship.

Language and learning

Yet clearly the quality of social interaction is now regarded as an important element in good teaching. While still maintaining the belief that children need to construct their own understanding of events, effective practitioners recognise the importance of language to the child's cognitive processes. The work of Bruner and Vygotsky in this field will be discussed in Chapter 5 when we examine cognition and teaching. Their influence is certainly evident in the current emphasis on what Walkerdine and Sinha (1978) describe as 'discourse formats', for example in science and mathematics.

Assessment of Performance Unit teams examining children's performance in science and language tasks found direct links between levels of performance, with use of language a crucial aspect. They argue that:

the view of 'language structure' as something wider and more coherent than word or single concepts is coming to be recognised as increasingly important to the way children cope with or fail to meet the demands of different school subjects (White, 1988, p.5).

Making a similar point the Cockcroft Report states:
Language plays an essential part in the formation and expression of mathematical ideas (DES, 1982, para. 306).

Language specialists also emphasise language use and the matching of discourse to context. Talking in terms of assessment the Kingman Committee stated:

We recognise . . . the notion that crucial features of language used relate to the specific situation and the precise task undertaken whatever the subject and that one cannot infer that a different task will produce the same kind of response (DES, 1988c, p. 57).

Children have to master considerable complexities of language use. It would appear that interaction with adults is an essential part of this process.

If children are to learn, that is construct meaning, in interaction with adults, the quality of that interaction is all important. Children need to use language appropriately and teachers need to see them do so. This exercise calls for the kind of relationship that Habermas was suggesting when he indicated that the ideal interaction was based on mutual respect and trust.

Talking with children

Nowhere is the need for these qualities more evident than in the diagnostic setting. The study of infant school children's learning experiences by Bennett *et al.* (1984) revealed that teachers found diagnosis of children's learning needs difficult to organise. They tended to put their felt need to be constantly available to all children above the importance of spending a few minutes in conversation with individual children. This certainly appears to hark back to their perceptions of Piaget's readiness principle and the implied dangers of missing that 'golden moment' of readiness to learn. In their study Bennett and his colleagues noted that because time spent in one-to-one conversation was so rare for children, when it actually occurred it proved to be of little use. Teachers seemed to have clear goals for the children they were talking with but rather than finding out how the child understood the task, the interviews tended to become question and answer testing sessions in which frequently the child was forced into the position of mind reader trying to ascertain the teacher's expectations.

Donaldson (1978) cautioned teachers to be wary of the power they hold over children in interactions, since children will consequently try to guess the adult's intentions in order to please, with the result that a distorted picture of what the child actually understands may emerge. High quality interactions on the other hand are premised on the teacher's need to know how the child is making sense of an experience. This information can only be elicited if it is to be received in a non-judgemental fashion with genuine interest in order to be used as a starting point for further teaching. The power framework mentioned by Donaldson is, of course, all pervasive and is sustained in the child's mind by experiences in all aspects of classroom life.

It is particularly evident in the relative frequency of teacher and pupil questions. Wood (1988) reports two studies, one of British pre-school children and the other of American high-school students. In these studies the frequency of teacher questions as a percentage of all utterances was 47 per cent in the British study and 43 per cent in the American investigation. By contrast children's questions accounted for 4 per cent and 8 per cent of utterances respectively. Indeed teacher questions seemed to inhibit child talk; the more frequently the teacher asked questions, the less the pupils talked about the topic, asked questions or talked to each other. It seemed that teachers were controlling through questioning and not permitting authentic dialogues.

Yet teachers appear to value the use of questions to encourage children's thinking and understanding. Brown and Edmondson (1984) found that this was the most frequently given reason for questions by their sample of teachers of 11 to 13 year-olds. The most commonly used types of questions were selected to elicit simple deductions or comparisons and to encourage recall, for example of procedures or knowledge. Both categories of questions would tend to arise in situations where the child would feel that the teacher was expecting the right answer. Clearly the skills of diagnosis call for subtlety and a conducive classroom ethos.

Negotiating for control

An attempt to analyse classroom life to enable the examination of interactions in different contexts has been carried out by Doyle in the United States. Taking the idea of negotiation between teacher and pupil as central to the avoidance of chaos in classrooms he has provided a useful framework for understanding classroom interactions. This will be elaborated in terms of children's learning and classroom management in Chapters 5 and 6. The teacher's concern, he argues, is to maintain order so that learning can occur. At the same time the pupil's concern is to avoid risk taking so that teacher approval is likely. Doyle (1983, 1986) observes that tasks which call for high level cognitive processes such as reasoning or problem solving tend to appear ambiguous to pupils who in turn try to avoid risk by demanding more detailed explanation and guidance. If teachers do not respond, pupil disruption may occur with the result that teachers may decide to eliminate these high risk tasks at the outset.

Doyle's analysis is useful because it allows us to see classroom life as a process of negotiation in which both participant groups, pupils and teachers, are to an extent vulnerable. From this perspective we cannot really understand classroom interaction unless we see the teacher's need to control as clearly as the child's need to please. In the 1986 review he proposes that both under- and over-control on the part of the teacher is non-conducive to challenging children into thinking and advocates an intermediate level in which teachers and pupils interact frequently to sustain order so that potential disorder is eradicated before it matures. He therefore sees effective pupil teacher interaction as crucial to creating the learning environment.

This belief is supported in a British study by French and Peskett (1986). They pointed out that any worthwhile interaction between pupils and teacher 'presupposes' order and attention. They observe that teacher control instructions are most frequently mitigated by the use of 'pleases' or endearments of the type used by Paul's teacher in the earlier illustration in this chapter.[1] Teachers are bidding for control and minimising their risks of public failure by maintaining a conversational, invitational mode.[2]

Teachers therefore have a fine balancing act to sustain when undertaking diagnostic questioning. At one level they need to demonstrate the respect they have for children's construction of experiences in order to base their teaching on the child's current level of understanding. At another level they need to maintain the order necessary for an effective learning environment. In the continuous process of negotiation that appears to occur in classrooms they have to be seen to be successful. If diagnostic questioning demands that children become more equal partners in negotiations across all aspects of classroom life, then teachers may feel that they are taking risks. Doyle suggests that tensions of this type are resolved through an increased emphasis on general classroom management. By setting up durable well-defined work systems for pupils, teachers establish a substructure of order against which negotiations are enacted. In effect, warm and democratic classroom climates which are conducive to effective learning depend upon carefully designed and controlled infrastructures of appropriate pupil tasks. The effective setting of these tasks, in turn depends upon accurate diagnosis of pupils' starting points for learning. These points will be elaborated in Chapter 6.

Pupil–pupil interaction

Interactions with teachers may be the most problematic for pupils (e.g. Edwards, 1988) but pupils also interact with each other. This interaction may not always be to their academic advantage. Wheldall, *et al.* (1981) compared the on-task behaviour of 11-year-old children when seated in rows and at tables and found that time on task was greater when the children were seated in rows facing the teacher. Wheldall (1985) pre-empts any simplistic interpretations of these data, suggesting that tables may prove more suitable for topic work or small group discussions. A similar study by Bennett and Blundell (1983) found that the quantity of children's work increased while they were seated in rows while the quality remained constant across rows and tables.

These studies tell us a great deal about the way group work has been perceived in primary classrooms since the Plowden Report (CACE, 1967). In the report, grouping was encouraged as a way of providing stage-related teaching within the time constraints existing in classrooms. Side benefits would include the advantages of learning from each other and the social experience of working alongside their peers. Within these parameters it was hardly surprising that grouping became a convenience of classroom management rather than an opportunity to explore the supposed benefits of collaborative learning. Studies by Boydell (1975), Tann (1981), Bennett (1985a) all suggest that cooperative group work rarely features in British primary school classrooms. Bennett summarises the state of group work when he states 'pupils work *in* groups but not *as* groups'.

This may be in part due to the belief that younger children are held back from collaboration by their egocentricity. However, as a result of a small-scale study with top infant children Hockaday (1984), pointed out that what inhibited effective collaboration was a restricted range of verbal strategies and limited reasoning and evaluating skills. This suggests that skills for interactive group work may be taught to young learners.

Yeomans (1983), in a research report on collaborative group work in primary and secondary schools, implies that the effort might be worthwhile. A feature of the American research, she notes, is that collaborative group work is particularly effective when attempting tasks demanding high level cognitive processes i.e. greater risks in Doyle's (1983) terms. Personal and social development also appear to be enhanced. Mutual concern develops, relationships across racial backgrounds are improved and positive feelings towards school are increased. Yeomans does observe that there is limited empirical evidence to support these claims. This qualification is also raised by Bennett who suggests that the field of group processes and learning has much to offer researchers (Bennett, 1985a). It may be timely for social and cognitive psychologists themselves to collaborate in interactive cooperative research groups.[3]

To return to the control issue raised by Doyle's work (Doyle, 1986), collaborative group work does take immediate control of events away from the teacher and calls for a form of interaction between pupil and teacher in which the teaching emphasis is on process rather than product and where judgements on process are made by the collaborating pupils as they constantly evaluate and adapt their responses to the task. Responsibility for the evaluation of process and outcome is clearly an element to be considered when pupil–teacher interaction occurs. As Edwards (1988) has argued, when teachers recognise pupils' rights to self-evaluation the possibility of an interaction which may truly inform teachers about pupils' learning is more likely.

Teachers' perceptions of children

Teachers' perceptions of children have long been recognised as variables to be considered in teaching (e.g. Salmon and Claire, 1984). Kelly's theory of personal constructs (Kelly, 1955; Bannister and Fransella, 1971) gives us a useful framework for examining the way our anticipations guide our behaviours. Arguing that we enter any interaction with expectations based upon previous experience and with a set of limited and personal criteria against which we evaluate the other person, Kelly provides us with a way of understanding the constraints we place on others and ourselves. This model also suggests that it is possible to break the cycle in which anticipations limit future experiences, but to do so may take some conscious effort on the part of the individual.

As we have pointed out in Chapter 2, areas where expectations based on cultural consensus may be detrimental to children include race, and gender. Tomlinson (1984) reviews British research on teacher expectations of Asian and West Indian pupils and their parents and concludes that teachers tend to hold 'very negative expectations' for the behaviour and academic potential of West Indian pupils, for example they were regarded as being more aggressive, the boys were more likely to be reported as 'behaviourally deviant' and their parents as less inclined to be concerned about their children's schooling. The Rampton Committee (DES, 1981) was clearly concerned that these attitudes towards pupils were unlikely to be conducive to academic progress.

Research into teacher attitudes to girls reveals a comparable state of affairs. Pratt (1985) reports the result of a survey of secondary school teacher attitudes to equal opportunities in school. The survey reveals that nearly half his sample of over 850 teachers appear to be unsympathetic towards equality of opportunity for pupils. Whyte (1983) argues that an even greater challenge faces primary schools. She points out that girls 'learn to lose' while at primary school, and as a result need 'specific encouragement to become more independent, assured, intrepid and equipped to deal with secondary and further or higher education'. She points out that the comfortable world of the primary school where the conformity of girls is expected and welcomed only encourages girls to please adults and avoid the risk taking often necessary in learning. Similarly Dweck's study of learned helplessness (Dweck *et al.*, 1978) reported that teachers accounted for the poor performances of girls in terms of 'intellectual inadequacies' while they attributed boys' low performances to poor motivation. That is, the girls were seen as innately incapable and unlikely to improve while the boys might be worth some perseverance to improve motivation and hence performance. This view of female passivity in primary schools is corroborated by Walden and Walkerdine (1985) when they note that primary school girls linked being good at their work with being a nice, kind and helpful person. It appears that primary school teachers, because of their need continuously to occupy and manage thirty or more lively individuals, expect and aim for conformity and passivity in their pupils and as both Whyte and Walden and Walkerdine point out, direct much of their energy to controlling and motivating the boys who they expect to be greater risk takers. Responding to challenge does not seem to be a major anticipation when teachers consider the girls in their classes. While this means that girls tend to perform better than boys at the primary school stage it is highly probable that problems are being stored up for their later educational experiences.

These issues are important because children learn about themselves in interaction with others. Teachers are a particularly powerful source of information about the self, or personal identity, for young children since they may be regarded as 'significant others' (Mead, 1934). Harré (1983) has usefully described personal identity as an important organising principle. In this sense children's actions are directed by their sense of self-efficacy which in turn may be determined by what the child feels she or he is allowed to do. To limit that sense by clinging to the constraints of stereotyping is to restrict the range of options of behaviour open to the child and so limit learning and development.

Tajfel (1978) makes some interesting comments on the phenomenon of the stereotype. He observes that the less information one holds about a person the more likely it is that group-related characteristics are assigned to that person. This may be relatively harmless if it is merely a way of flexibly classifying someone until more information is available. However, if there is an 'emotional charge', which may be fed by strong prejudices, then stereotypes tend to be rigid and not amenable to change.

Again the value of a real information seeking dialogue in which children's perspectives are received non-judgementally by teachers would seem one way of recasting role stereotypes more flexibly. While emotionally charged rigid stereotypes may be hard to deal with, the role of the school in providing information and encouraging cross-cultural interaction to prevent the construction of such prejudices is evident.

The control dimension

It seems that it is impossible to get away from the tension that lies at the root of pupil-teacher interaction. Effective teachers recognise that equal and open communication with pupils is conducive to the accurate diagnosis of needs which is essential to their planning of tasks. They are aware that tasks which entail cognitive challenge tend to involve risk taking and that this may lead to insecurity, fear of teacher judgement and avoidance strategies on the part of children. Equally they know that order and control over incipient chaos is a pre-requisite to any teaching and learning and as a result they appear to place the control need over the communication need. As we stated earlier, interactions are in part determined by the contexts in which they occur. Control is clearly important as teachers have the day-to-day responsibility for the safety and general discipline of their pupils. In addition they teach alongside colleagues who expect order. In the private world of primary school teaching a slip in classroom control is far more immediately evident than errors in curriculum planning.

It would be pessimistic to assume that these factors necessarily militate against good classroom interactions. A more positive step is to examine ways in which the quality of interaction may be improved within existing contexts.

Improving the quality of interaction

If we take the ideal model of teacher-pupil interaction to be one of mutual regard in which the child feels assured that his or her contributions are valued, we need to examine teaching strategies which will permit the child to enter the dialogue armed with a sense of his or her own rights and responsibilities. This kind of interaction, as we have already argued, is impossible to achieve when the child feels that the teacher's prime concern is hearing the one correct answer. The processes of classroom interaction have to be consistent. Children may find it difficult to take creative risks in problem solving tasks when in the previous science session that day teacher evaluations of their responses had dominated. Several strategies need to be employed simultaneously to ensure the appropriate classroom ethos if the desired dialogue is to take place.

1. The self-evaluating pupil

Nisbet and Shucksmith (1986) start their examination of children's learning strategies with the assertion that learning how to learn is in fact the most important learning. Drawing on the notion of metacognition or an awareness of one's own mental process, they argue that to recognise and manage task demands is essential to successful learning. Usefully taking this idea to classroom practice they discuss learning strategies which they consider to be 'higher order skills' which monitor the use of the lower order practical skills demanded by the task. These strategies are outlined in more detail in Chapter 5.

Brown and De Loache (1983) make a similar claim for the importance of what they term metacognitive skills or behaviour for 'co-ordinating and controlling' learning. They emphasise the transferability of these skills across the child's learning experiences to the extent that they should be applied whenever a new task is met.

Both pairs of psychologists argue that these strategies should be taught in schools. Acquisition has the effect of freeing the child from the need to constantly seek teacher approval. Once goals have been clearly established the child should be responsible for monitoring his or her progress towards those goals. There are of course implications for pupil-teacher interactions during that progress as the teacher has to stand back and allow pupil decision-making to proceed.

2. Asking questions

Bruner (1974) has argued that children's questions reveal more about their understanding than do their answers. At another level, Nisbet and Shucksmith (1986) consider asking questions about the task to be an important learning strategy. Teachers' responses to children's questions provide the key to the quality of the interaction. Taking diagnosis as a starting point for teaching it may be appropriate to respond with a question which explores the way that the child is making sense. Those questions demanding further information, for example 'what if . . . ?' or 'what would happen next?', are useful. Equally, encouraging the process of learning how to learn may necessitate bouncing the question back to the child for the required evaluation for example, 'what do you think?'. To create an ethos in which true, undistorted communication can occur it is necessary to attend to the type and use of teacher questions and to allow some control to the child.

3. Valuing process

A prerequisite to the notion of 'independent learner' and a corollary of the recognition of the power of teacher questions is a need to emphasise the processes that lead to task completion in order to provide a counterbalance to a focus on the quality of the final outcome. Any task set by teachers may make a range of demands on learners. Bennett *et al.* (1984) provide a useful introduction to the complexities of task analysis. Equally the strategies outlined by Nisbet and Shucksmith (1986) suggest it is possible to identify specific process skills which can be signalled to the child as important.

Once the 'how' as well as the 'what' of task completion is seen to be valued the child is to an extent, freed from problems of the finality of teacher judgements of outcomes and able to operate in a situation where teacher help with process skills may be requested without fear of failing to please.

4. The self-evaluating teacher

The suggestions made in this chapter for improving interaction in classrooms require considerable teacher self-awareness. To ensure that teacher questions are appropriate, that children are using their learning strategies independently or working effectively in groups, demands constant monitoring of classroom processes. Simple strategies such as tape recording oneself leading a class discussion, or placing a cassette recorder on a table where two children are engaged in a problem solving task will yield rich information on teaching styles and the contributions of pupils.

Effective teachers spend a lot of time listening to pupils. Within an interactionist model of pedagogy it is important that they are also aware of the cues, messages and opportunities that they present to pupils. The only way to achieve this is through careful monitoring of practice followed by self-reflection.

The aim of this activity is not to disempower or undermine the confidence of practitioners, though it can be a challenging experience. On the contrary, the self-evaluating teacher emerges from the experience strengthened by a greater understanding of his or her own pedagogy and with fresh insights into ways in which it might be developed. Stressing, as we do in this volume, the importance of the teacher to children's learning we are bound to emphasise the need for teachers to be alert to all elements of their own practice.

Suggestions for further reading

1. For a good introduction to social identity and the construction of identity, Pervin, L. (1984) Am I me or am I the situation? In P. Barnes, J. Oates, J. Chapman, V. Lee, and P. Czerniewska (eds).
    Personality Development and Learning. London, Hodder and Stoughton.
    For more challenging reading on this topic see:
    Harré R. (1979) *Social Being*. Oxford, Basil Blackwell.
    Harré R. (1983) *Personal Being*. Oxford, Basil Blackwell.
    Shotter, J. (1984) *Social Accountability and Selfhood*. Oxford, Basil Blackwell.

2. Issues of power and control in educational settings are well documented in the field of sociology of education – see for example:
    Apple M. (1979) *Ideology and Curriculum* London, Routledge and Kegan Paul.
    Apple, M. (1983) *Power and Education.* London, Routledge and Kegan Paul.
    Barton, L. and Meighan, R. (eds.) (1978) *Sociological Interpretations of Schooling and Classrooms: a reappraisal.* Driffield, Nafferton.
    Whitty, G. and Young. M. (eds) (1976) *Explorations in the Politics of School Knowledge.* Driffield, Nafferton.

Suggestions for seminar activities

1. Ask students to tape record themselves introducing a new 'object', e.g. a piece of equipment or a stimulus for fantasy play to two children: a boy and a girl. A few minutes of the recording should be transcribed and brought to the seminar. Extracts can be discussed in pairs or by the whole group to explore the distribution of power in interaction, how it was exercised and controlled and the implications for the student's own model of how children best learn.

    This recording can be used for similar exercises to explore ideas raised in Chapters 5 and 6.
2. Ask students to distinguish the rules and rituals of the seminar. What are their purposes? How are they played? How are they learnt? How might it be done better? What are the implications for classroom teaching? Why do teachers work in the way they do? How might it be done better?

CHAPTER 5

How do children make sense of the information around them?

Making sense of school

Let us return to Jenny and Paul in their first few weeks at school. As they move around the classroom, the playground and the other areas of the school they have a wide range of experiences and see and hear a vast amount. Yet it is almost certain that they will make sense of their experiences and the information around them in their own and different ways. When listening to an adult tell a story they may connect the events to a more familiar version of the narrative or perhaps to similar real-life events of their own. While playing with small building blocks they may sort by size or build a house, guided by what they each regard the purpose of the blocks to be. In this situation the major function of the teacher is to ensure that children pay attention to those aspects of classroom life which offer optimal learning experiences.

Doyle (1986) has described classrooms as confusing places in which both pupils and teachers negotiate order out of incipient chaos. Part of this confusion, he explains, lies in the extensive array of stimuli which compete for a child's attention, blocks which may be used for sorting, counting, building or throwing, being only one small part of that choice. At the very least it would seem to be the teacher's role to help children to make appropriate selections from this array. During the course of this chapter we will suggest that the teacher's role extends beyond this, as Doyle (1983) has argued, to involve a sophisticated understanding of children and of the tasks provided. This claim is no more than an attempt to clarify the relationship between theories of how children make sense of their worlds and what is sometimes elusively labelled good primary practice.

As Jenny and Paul start school they take their first step into the institutionalised citizen-creating process we call schooling. From whatever political perspective we view education systems there would be little dispute over that statement (e.g. Apple, 1985; Walkerdine, 1984). Pupils are expected to acquire the skills, concepts and attitudes of the prevailing culture. The implementation of a national curriculum is current testimony to that. There is nothing unusual in this expectation of education; Cole (1985) is one of many psychologists who take a cross-cultural perspective to demonstrate how, even in relatively primitive societies, the role of the adult is to instruct the child into ways of maintaining existing cultural competencies and priorities.

However, teaching in school is probably more problematic than, for example, the apprenticeship situation among the Zinacantecan weavers of Mexico described by Cole. Teaching has evolved into a professional occupation which involves engagement with the processes of pedagogy. Although it may be difficult to describe a commonly held and articulated model of primary school pedagogy it is likely that there would be some agreement on the need for the child to become an effective and independent learner. That this statement may, in fact, be based on a range of assumptions about teaching and learning and hence used to support a variety of forms of pedagogy will be evident in the course of this chapter. This ambivalence is of little help to the teaching profession at a time when the lack of a coherent view of effective pedagogy has rendered it vulnerable to curriculum design backed by legislation. Psychology has either not always served the profession well (Donaldson, 1978; Walkerdine, 1984) or appears to have had little impact on teachers (Zeichner *et al.*, 1987). Nevertheless, our belief is that effective teaching can be underpinned by a clear model of children's learning. Further, if teaching is to be regarded as more than a mechanistic exercise that model needs to be understood by teachers to the extent that it informs their day-to-day classroom decision making.

The Piagetian inheritance

The insights provided by Piaget's research into the ways that children make sense of their environment are considerable. His major contributions were, (a) to focus the attention of primary teachers on to the possibility that children at different stages of cognitive development were interpreting experiences in different ways from adults, and (b) to provide an explanatory model of the learning process which still holds water as one of the 'best bets' available.

While not dwelling either on the intricacies of each stage of development (see Table 5.1) or on the extensive critique of his work (Donaldson, 1978; Brown and Desforges, 1979), the notion of stages focused attention on the developing mental structures of the child and the importance of matching learning experiences to the child's ability to cope with them; this has been a crucially important stimulus to the development of current pedagogy. As we can see from Table 5.1, it has also provided a justification for the age structure of the British School System. (See Shayer and Adey, 1981 for a useful critique of ages and stages.)

Table 5.1 **Piaget's stages of development as they relate to Schooling**

I	The Sensori-Motor Period (Infancy)
II	The Pre-operational Period (Preschool and infant school)
III	The Concrete Operative Period (Junior schools)
IV	The Formal Operations Period (Secondary schooling)

Similarly the explanatory mechanisms Piaget provided to demonstrate the processes of learning have had far-reaching consequences for primary practice. Understanding these processes necessitates getting to grips with the terms 'assimilation' and 'accommodation' (see Table 5.2)

Table 5.2 **Piaget's intellectual processes**

Assimilation
The organism (mind) deals with new events by making them fit into its existing structures. The organism does not adapt itself to the new information. This needs to be balanced by some form of:

Accommodation
The organism (mind) adapts to the new events, for example, new concepts are formed or existing ones extended to incorporate and make sense of the new information.

In addition to emphasising the importance of play for assimilation purposes and careful sequencing of experience to ensure accommodation, this model places the child actively at the centre of his or her own learning.

The prominence accorded Piaget's work enabled practitioners to see children as active learners who construct models of the world using the mental processes of which they are developmentally capable. The effect on pedagogy was to encourage adults to look at and listen to children and to consider the appropriateness of the learning experiences provided. Another equally important point implicit in his biological model of child development was a view of intelligence as intelligent behaviour, or appropriate adaptation to one's environment. His work was instrumental in making a case for the psychological foundations of pedagogy and has provided new generations of developmental and cognitive psychologists with a field of study in which psychological knowledge can have important practical applications.

Theories of child development and theories of instruction

The heart of the educational process consists of providing aids and dialogues for translating experience into more powerful systems of notation and ordering. And it is for this reason that I think a theory of development must be linked to both a theory of knowledge and to a theory of instruction, or be doomed to triviality (Bruner, 1966, p. 21).

The assumptions within this statement are profound and need to be addressed if pedagogy is to be regarded as something more than enhancing the 'natural' developmental processes of the child. First, we need to assume that what the teacher does may affect the success of the child's learning and, secondly, that what is to be learnt needs to be understood by the adult to the extent that she or he is able to order and organise the experiences or information to be tackled by the child.

The belated translation of Vygotsky's work into English (e.g. Vygotsky, 1962 and Vygotsky, 1978) has provided educationalists with an alternative to Piagetian theory. Whereas the Piagetian model of children's thinking would explain a child's inability to handle new information or tasks simply as lack of maturity in their intellectual structures, the framework supplied by Vygotskian theory would allow us to see the failure to cope both in developmental terms and in terms of a lack of relevant prior experiences with a consequent inability to make appropriate connections to existing knowledge. The fundamental difference between the two views is that while Piagetian theory allows educationalists to talk of the 'natural' development of the child's cognitive structures the Vygotskian perspective places the 'teacher' firmly alongside the child in a process of jointly constructing meaning and so emphasises the importance of language and communication in the construction of an understanding of the world.[1]

Let us again consider Jenny and Paul. Whatever their home circumstances, already they will have learnt a great deal before starting school. Research with mothers and infants shows how early and how much babies learn. Trevarthen (1977) describes the human infant as 'highly competent' and endowed with 'potentialities for psychological action'. These potentialities are initially enhanced in interaction with the care-giver. Infants are able to respond to adult behaviour. The 'turn taking' that is observed can be considered to be a form of proto-conversation or pre-speech (Trevarthen, 1974). Moving on to consider the infant's entry into the accumulated knowledge we describe as culture, Newson (1977) argues that adults induct infants into the significant aspects of their culture by highlighting what is relevant and important through dialogues and other forms of interaction.

An example of these processes at work in early numeracy has been documented by Saxe, Guberman and Gearhart (1987) in their study of the social interactions of 2 1/2 to 4 1/2 year-olds with their mothers.

Their data suggest that children's early numerical experiences form part of a system of social negotiation which is linked to both their own previous learning experiences and to the input of the social and cultural context in which these negotiations occur.

At the centre of this interactive view of learning is the notion of infant and child intentionality, as conversations or interactions imply some intentionality on both sides. We have already noted in Chapter 4 that in early infancy adults act as if the child has intentions in order to induct him or her into a dialogue with the adult who mediates the culture.

In terms of cognitive competence this intentionality is perhaps best observed in the child's search for meaning. Bruner (1986) summarises a decade of his research on infant-adult interactions as a search for the theories that adults and infants build about each other. Here he follows the argument that people need to build models and to categorise events in order to be able to predict the outcomes of behaviour, i.e. we develop theories about kinds of people, kinds of problems, kinds of human conditions. The origins of these categorisations lie in the culture in which we grow up. The role of the adult in this view of learning is to bring the child to the categorisation processes that are used in that culture. The role of the teacher is to select from the culture those skills or concepts which the child both needs and has the necessary experience to acquire.

Bruner again summarises this process when he describes mental growth as something

dependent upon growth from the outside in, a mastery of techniques that are embodied in the culture and that are passed on in a contingent dialogue by agents of the culture (Bruner, 1966. p. 21).

How does the child make sense?

So far we have described the context in which learning best occurs and have suggested that children are actively engaged in a process of constructing meaning or categorising the information they perceive. Humans try to make sense of new information by relating it to what they already know and by trying to fit it into their pre-existing information categories. If the information does not fit easily, the categories may need to be altered in order to accommodate the new information.

Young children tend to operate with over-extended categories. Thus Gruendel (1977) reports how 'Stephen' developed a concept of 'hatness' which included anything which could be put on a head; as he acted upon an object by placing it on his head it became a hat, whether it was a book or a bucket, he then progressed to exclude those items which did not have an enclosure, so keys and books were no longer labelled as hats. Eventually the construct was narrowed to match that operated by adults. Of course one has to be tentative in ascribing too much to observations of this kind as young children have very limited vocabularies and therefore may have greater understanding than they are able to express in words.

The relationship between language and the construction of meaning is not easy to tease out. Nelson (1977) points to the connection between language and making sense when she describes concept formation and naming as 'a first manifestation of a continuing process of stabilising an inherently unstable experience in order to operate on it and make predictions about it'. The teacher's concern, as we have already said, is to enable the child to acquire the category system used by adult members of society. As Wells (1981, p. 81) indicates, this is not a simple task. The child's organisation of concepts does not necessarily fit that of adults and the child's organisation is anyway constantly open to change as a result of new experiences.

Mathematics education is one area where the necessity to give children entry into specific form of discourse is obvious. The Open University course Developing Mathematical Thinking (EM 235) (Floyd, 1981) has produced a useful pedagogical framework which complements the explanation of the relationship between language and thinking supplied by Wells. Taking 'Doing, Talking and Recording' as key stages in mathematical activities, Floyd emphasises the importance of 'talk about doing' as the vital link between the doing and the recording. The language associated with the doing allows the children to reflect, make connections and extrapolate. Brissenden (1988) provides helpful guidelines for setting up activities within the framework of 'Do, Talk and Record' and emphasises the importance of learner-teacher interaction during the doing phase when the child is also encouraged to record information using his or her own informal methods as a precursor to taking on the culturally accepted notations at a later date.

A key concern for educators therefore, has to be the role of language in constructing meaning. The Gruendel observations mentioned earlier suggest that meaning is constructed both through action and by using language to label or categorise. In Stephen's case this was achieved by exploring the function of hatness and by labelling objects as 'hat' with an implied category of 'not hat'.

Wells (1981, p. 81) gives a useful explanation of the process that may be at work:

existing concepts providing a clue to the meanings of words heard, and words heard lead to a modification of existing concepts, with the situational context in both cases providing additional support in establishing the relationship on particular occasions (Wells, 1981, p. 81).

However, he does proceeed to make the case for the overall importance of language, as once it is acquired it 'becomes a means of extending the range and complexity of thought' (p. 87). Linguistic representations appear to release children from the here and now to enable them to extrapolate, make connections and construct their own meaning systems.

The role of the adult

The interplay between language and action in the construction of meaning would certainly suggest that adult and child need to work alongside each other for at least part of the child's learning process.

Vygotsky (1978) has provided teachers with a useful model of teacher–pupil roles in what he describes as school learning. He suggests that when we make a judgement about a child's intellectual capacity we must examine two developmental levels. The first is the 'actual developmental level' of the child and is assessed on what the child can do now as a result of previous learning. The second level, the level of potential development, is assessed on the basis of what the child is able to do after careful teaching. Vygotsky argued that indications of the child's ability to learn from others were more revealing than a measure based upon the previous learning achieved by the child, as the latter might simply reflect the developmental opportunities available. The difference between the actual developmental level and the level of potential development he termed the zone of proximal development (ZPD). The ZPD is more than a diagnostic model. Vygotsky saw it in pedagogical terms, as developmental processes internal to the child are triggered to come into operation when the child interacts with the adults who mediate or pass on the culture. As a consequence the child's learning has to be structured by careful selection and organisation of information and experiences. Vygotsky's emphasis on the role of the teacher is explicit, as it is usually the interaction with adults which sets off internal changes in the child's mental construction of the world. The adult's role may be to introduce new ideas and information and then to provide the child with further opportunities to consolidate that new information and to make the necessary adjustments in his or her existing system of mental constructs. Indeed the model of mathematics learning explicit in the framework of 'Do, Talk and Record' (Floyd, 1981 and Brissenden, 1988), described in the previous section, would be an example of Vygotskian theory in action. There the teacher interacts with the learner in the initial stages to provide information, to use language and to model skills before encouraging the child to incorporate these new elements into his or her own actions.

Matching task and child

The description of the pedagogic processes described by Vygotsky points to the degree of responsibility that the teacher holds for the child's learning. He writes:

properly organised learning results in mental development and sets in motion a variety of developmental processes that would be impossible apart from learning (Vygotsky, 1978, p. 90).

It is the 'proper organisation' of the learning that is the key. This implies careful diagnostic assessment of the child's existing category system and appropriate sequencing of learning experiences to move the child from that point towards the next defined curricular goal. Ausubel put it another way when he admonished teachers to find out 'where the child is at, and teach him accordingly' (Ausubel, 1968).

Matching the task to child at the very least therefore involves assessment of the child's existing ways of understanding events and his or her ability to deal with the new information, together with an analysis of the relevant curriculum in order to enable careful and appropriate sequencing of information or skills. The latter is as important as the former. Driver (1983) describes children's inadequate categorisation of scientific knowledge as 'alternative frameworks' and argues that teachers have to take these as their starting points with children while endeavouring to ensure that there is little opportunity for proliferation of such frameworks as they only provide obstacles to children's learning. Pointing out the improbability that children will 'discover' the models and conventions of current scientific thought, she proposes that a clear role for the teacher is to 'help children assimilate their practical experiences into what is possibly a new way of thinking about them' (Driver, 1983, p. 9).

Driver's work illustrates the two most evident aspects of match: the need to understand the learner and the need to know the sequence of skills and concepts relevant to a particular curriculum area. The work of Norman (1978) and a subsequent study by Bennett *et al.* (1984) suggest that the two-dimensional framework so far outlined is simply a starting point. Norman starts with the premise already discussed; that new information interacts with the learning in existing organised mental structures. Successful learning occurs when that new input is integrated with appropriate existing categories. He isolated three processes at work in the experience of learning: accretion, restructuring and tuning. Accretion is the first phase and may involve the child in the initial acquisition of facts or the introduction to skills. During the second phase, the existing category system is restructured to accommodate the new information and old information is provided with new insights from fresh input. During the final phase of learning, new skills and ways of understanding are fine-tuned or practised until they appear to be used 'automatically'. All three phases are essential to successful learning and although they may not be separated out into clearly distinct sequential phases their relative importance to the process of learning is in the sequence of accretion, restructuring and tuning just outlined.

This analysis of potential task demand can be of enormous help to teachers in the management of teaching time; for example the need for teacher input or monitoring decreases as the child moves from accretion which requires high teacher input to tuning or practice tasks. This supports the framework outlined by Floyd (1981) and Brissenden (1988). Moreover, it emphasises the complexity of learning processes and hence the intricacy of task analysis and design. Using this sequence, teachers can categorise tasks according to their appropriateness to the child's position in the learning cycle Norman provides. Bennett *et al.* (1984), used a modification of Norman's three-phase analysis to categorise language and mathematics tasks set for 7- and 8-year-olds. They found that only 40 per cent of tasks in English and Mathematics set for 7-year-olds and 30 per cent of those set for 8-year-olds actually challenged children, despite teachers' concern to achieve good 'match'. When the observations of Doyle are added to this analysis of task setting the situation becomes even more fraught. According to Doyle and Carter (1984) pupils and teachers engage in a process of negotiation around the setting and completion of tasks as part of the attempt to avoid the incipient chaos of classroom life. Children, they argue, try to reduce the risk of failure and consequent teacher displeasure by negotiating around the task until it can be seen as a set of routine activities. Moreover, teachers respond to pupil's bids or negotiations because of a similar need to maintain order and avoid chaos. Tasks are therefore modified and simplified to facilitate successful completion. The result is frequently an emphasis on routine responses. Bennett *et al.* (1984) found that more than half of the mathematical tasks they observed were mismatched to the children. Teachers tended to underestimate the ability of high attaining children and overestimate that of the low attainers. Bennett and his colleagues suggest that classroom management issues are at the centre of some aspects of mismatch. We shall be picking up these points again in Chapter 6.

What is most evident in the study by Bennett *et al.* (1984) is the inappropriate use of much learning time in classrooms. Teachers in their study were unable to find the time for diagnosis of pupil learning needs and lacked the skills for effective open-ended diagnostic assessment when they did. Yet if we are to return to Vygotsky and the ZPD mentioned earlier in this chapter, it would seem that these skills should be a central part of the professional repertoire of teachers.[2]

Using memories

Of course, as we have already asserted, there is more to match than diagnosis. Again we return to Vygotsky and his emphasis on the organisation of pupils' learning. It would seem that for information to be processed and stored the child has to be able to 'make sense' of it. Work on memory as a system of information processing and recall may help us to see the importance of sequencing and matching to the mental processing we term learning. Talking of adult learning, Craik and Tulving (1975) argued that the success of memory for items depended upon the degree to which they could be connected to other items already stored in the memory. Craik and Tulving were particularly concerned with what they termed the 'depth of processing' of information and suggested that information processing is facilitated by assisting the learner to make sense of new information by giving additional information about an item to be remembered. This assistance is termed 'elaboration' and its purpose seems to be to enable the learner to connect input to existing structures.[3]

In terms of teaching and learning it would seem that new information or skills need to be organised by teachers into manageable, relevant and carefully sequenced experiences for the learner. When dealing with children this is particularly problematic as the information store to which new inputs might be connected is more limited than that of most adults. Chi (1978 and 1981) argues that differences between adults and children in the ability to remember information are due largely to the fact that children have less content knowledge. Another element in the differences in processing is the fact that adults are more expert at using effective storage and retrieval strategies, that is they are better at organising information input.

The implications of Chi's work for teaching and learning are important. First, it enables teachers to regard children's limitations as learners as starting points for teaching. Children can be helped to become more expert in terms of content knowledge and in the organisation of their own learning. Secondly, and here we return to 'match', it emphasises the need to recognise that children do have limited knowledge bases, and the necessity to sequence learning experiences which take these limitations into account and enable the child to 'make sense' in accord with teacher intentions.

Learning strategies

Attention to organisation of the learning experiences to which the child is exposed would appear particularly important when dealing with novices, that is, when the learner has little expertise in the topic. Berliner (1987) differentiates between the information processing abilities of novices and experts by noting that while the expert can select what is important from information received, novices are unable to separate the important from the unimportant. It would therefore seem that the three-stage task model offered by Norman (1978) provides a useful way of perceiving the role of the teacher. Learner expertise may be augmented by careful organisation of input whether that input is information, language or skills, or more probably a combination of these. Important aspects of the new experience are necessarily highlighted by the 'expert' teacher and the child engages in a process of restructuring his or her existing storage system to accommodate the new information. He or she then progresses to integrate that information or skill to the extent that its use becomes 'automatic'. The two stages described by Norman as restructuring and practice may well be positioned within independent problem solving tasks set up by teachers. If we see problem solving tasks as appropriate vehicles for the child's internalisation of new experiences we need to recognise that it is important that the child is in charge of his or her own learning at this stage. The adjustments being made relate to the knowledge structures of each individual child. While the teacher has set the goals for learning, and limited the opportunity for error by carefully organising input and by appropriate task setting and resourcing, the learner has to 'make sense' for him or herself.

Teachers can, nevertheless, enhance the child's ability to make sense and make connections. Children can be taught to be better learners, better organisers of their own learning and better users of what they already know. At one level this is done through helping the child to see the need to organise learning, to select what is important and to regulate and control related actions. At another level it is possible to teach children to recognise their need to exercise specific learning strategies.

Nisbet and Shucksmith (1986) have isolated strategies necessary for effective learning. These strategies are seen as 'executive processes' which select, regulate and apply skills to suit the needs of the task. Nisbet and Shucksmith describe learning to learn as developing metacognitive awareness or cultivating a 'seventh sense': an appreciation of one's own mental processes. Crucially, they see the learners' ability to monitor task demands and to select appropriate skills to be at the core of effective learning. Taking the notion of 'planfulness' as the key construct they explain the importance of enhancing the learner's ability to ask questions related to task demand, to reduce the task to manageable components, to monitor, check and revise progress towards the goal and, interestingly, to self-evaluate. They argue that enhancing the learner's ability to reflect upon his or her own learning and to respond to self-evaluations is an important teaching task enabling the child to take responsibility for his or her own learning. The model of the self-evaluating learner is presented as a necessary partner to the self-evaluating teacher presented in earlier chapters.

To return to Jenny and Paul in the reception class, while they may be too young to cultivate the range of metacognitive strategies outlined by Nisbet and Shucksmith it is not inappropriate to build planning and self-review into the structure of sessions with relatively young learners as the actual processes of learning and making sense differ little between child and adult learner.

Notes and further reading

1. On Vygotskian approaches to children's learning, Andrew Sutton provides a good overview and introduction to Soviet Psychology in Sutton, A. (1983) An Introduction to Soviet Developmental Psychology. In S. Meadows (ed.) *Developing Thinking*. London, Methuen.
   These ideas are explored in greater depth in several papers in Wertsch J.V. (ed.) (1985) *Culture Communication and Cognition: Vygotskian Perspectives*. Cambridge, Cambridge University Press.
2. Examples of the British developmental, interactional view of children's learning in and out of school is found in papers by Paul Light, David Wood, Peter Robinson and Chris Hensall and Jacqueline McGuire in Richards, M. and Light P. (eds) (1986) *Children of Social Worlds*. Cambridge, Polity Press.
   At a more specific level, Michael Beveridge's collection of papers on language and thought is challenging and still to be bettered. Beveridge, M. (ed.) (1982) *Children Thinking Through Language*. London, Edward Arnold.
3. In the area of memory an interesting approach has been taken by David Middleton and Derek Edwards as they examine remembering and forgetting as socially constituted. Middleton, D. and Edwards, D. (eds) (1990) *Collective Remembering*. London, Sage.

Suggestions for seminar activities

1. Ask students to think of a typical primary classroom task that they have recently set a group of children, or would consider appropriate for a group.
   (a) Categorise this task as high or low risk – e.g. was it open-ended? Were the goals clear? Were children able to evaluate their performance in the task? What was your role in task setting and evaluating their outcomes? What are the implications for planning and setting tasks?
   (b) Categorise this task according to the three levels of task demand offered by Norman (1978). What preceded it, what followed it? Is there a match between your task setting and Norman's framework? What are the implications for planning tasks and assessing children's performances?
2. Ask students to tape record themselves introducing a new object or materials to a boy and a girl. They may use the recording made for the activity suggested at the end of Chapter 4. Students should bring transcribed extracts from this recording to share at the seminar. Use these extracts to explore each student's own implicit theory of how children

learn, for example: How important is language? How are children inducted into appropriate language use? What is the role of the adult? What theories of how children learn guide their actions as teachers? What proof do they have that these are useful theories?

3. Ask students to think of something they have completed recently, for example an essay, a sweater, a meal for friends. Ask them to analyse both the task-specific skills, for example holding a pen, doing cable stitch, and the more general skills, for example clarifying aims, organising materials. Students should then compare the general skills across tasks (reference to Nisbet and Shucksmith, 1986, would be helpful here) and then discuss ways in which these may be taught in primary schools.

4. Ask students to examine carefully the two extended quotations from Bruner (1966) to be found in the section 'Theories of Child Development and Theories of Instruction' in this chapter. Discuss the implications of these statements for the role of the primary teacher.

CHAPTER 6

Classroom management

Keeping chaos at bay?

While our two reception class children, Jenny and Paul, are endeavouring to make sense of their initial experiences of school their teacher is faced with a seemingly impossible balancing act. She needs to ensure that each child is motivated and confident enough to engage in constructing understandings of both the rituals of schooling and the official curriculum and at the same time she has to hold together these mentally and physically active individuals as a cohesive and manageable group and succeed in facilitating their learning of a particular and prescribed body of knowledge and skills. If that were not enough, external sanctions are at work. At the very least she must avoid having 'a noisy class', or forever be an uncomfortable reminder to colleagues of the incipient chaos in every classroom. Additionally she must effectively carry the school's national curriculum baton over the hurdles of appropriate levels of attainment. How does she manage it all?

Central to effective management is the ability to get the best from oneself and from others. When this maxim is applied to classrooms, the concern has to be use of pupil and teacher time so that children are able to learn efficiently and effectively. In other words, classroom management issues may start as questions about resources, uses of space and time and groupings of pupils but at essence lies a concern with effective teaching and learning.

Models of classroom management will therefore reflect pedagogical practices. There is a process of double reflection at work here as equally pedagogical practices may be produced by models of classroom management, for example lift-top sloping desks placed in rows do not lend themselves to practical group work activities, however much the teacher may wish to work in that way. Teachers have a range of management options available, though the choice is not always a free one, as schools develop particular styles into which pupils are inducted and within which the teaching staff are expected, by parents, pupils and colleagues to operate.[1]

The methods of management available in primary classrooms are used in varying degrees by most teachers and these both underpin and are underpinned by what is generally considered to be good primary practice. Three key issues which emerge from the literature are: surveillance, busyness and negotiation.

Surveillance

The origins of the idea of teacher as facilitator and monitor of children's learning can be found within the two major elements of British primary education. The first is summarised as education for social control and could be seen, in its prime, in the large classes of the old elementary schools in which the teacher armed with a cane and supported by the monitorial system controlled the behaviour of the children of the economically poorer social classes. The second element has its provenance in the child-centred view of children's learning and development. Here the teacher observed pupils, ever watchful for the moment of their 'readiness' for the next appropriate learning experience. Observation skills provided the only access to children's development as it was feared that questioning at inappropriate times in the child's stage of development could confuse and demotivate. The marriage of these two, apparently contradictory strands has been cogently traced by Valerie Walkerdine (1984) who argues that as both have at essence the notion of normalisation, whether it be becoming a fit and normal member of society or moving at appropriate speed through a progression of predetermined stages to a normal or expected understanding of events, their synthesis within a system of schooling is not that surprising.

Certainly the power of the surveyor is sustained only by his or her ability to see what is going on and hence to deny the right of private activity to the other actors, so ensuring that order and official purposes are maintained. The surveillance model can only be operated within classrooms in which an interactive pedagogy is dominant if the teacher engages in careful organisation of space, resources and time. The teacher needs to be able to observe each child at work with at best a sweep of the head or at most movement by a few paces. Resources need to be organised and positioned so that self-selection by children may be noted even at a distance, and time needs to be apportioned to groups of children in blocks which ensure that monitoring of some groups may occur while more intensive teaching is going on with others.

Another feature of the surveillance method of management is whole-class teaching which, in terms of current 'good practice', does not necessarily mean teacher exposition and an expectation of uniform pupil response. The present preferred model involves an introduction of topic or tasks to a whole class or relatively large group followed by children's activity on carefully resourced tasks and a class or group review session. In this way children are directed to tasks and held accountable through the review for their progress or outcomes. This method of organisation is validated by a model of learning which emphasises the role of the teacher in structuring and organising children's learning experiences as they are channelled into a specific curriculum.

Busyness

Like the monitoring of children, the prevalence of 'busyness' in primary school classrooms is a result of the syntheses of two apparently contradictory elements in the development of primary practice. The first strand has its roots in the emphasis placed on 'work' within protestant culture. The high moral value accorded the work ethic is best summarised in the fear of the fun the devil might have with idle-handed children. Schooling with its role in ensuring the moral well-being of the poorer classes clearly had to ensure that the sin of idleness was not evident. The second starting point, apparently in stark contrast to the first, is found in the belief in childhood innocence underpinning the progressive movement of the 1930s eventually taken up in the Plowden Report (CACE, 1967). In this strand, the child's natural curiosity is believed to motivate him or her to act upon the world and so learn. This is supported by a theory of effectiveness motivation (White, 1959) which argues that children are motivated to undertake tasks at which they feel they will be effective. As a result, children's natural behaviour is channelled into a specific curriculum through appropriate matching of task to child. Evidence of successful task setting is seen in the 'busyness' of the child as she or he is engaged on a task. In both strands the child's engagement with a classroom task is a visible sign of teacher success in managing children.

In terms of the reality of coping with the learning needs of thirty or more children, task setting and children's time on task are crucial classroom management issues, since unoccupied children are poised to trigger the incipient chaos of classroom life already discussed in Chapter 5. Teachers tend to organise their teaching day as a series of tasks or pupil activities. Nevertheless, in their study of task allocation and matching of task and child in top infant classes and first-year junior classes, Bennett *et al.* (1984) found that the 'experienced and able' teachers they observed had problems in achieving appropriate match. The research team also noted mismatch was caused by both underestimation as well as overestimation. A simple measure of time on task may give some indication of a teacher's success as manager of children. But as Bennett and Blundell (1983) point out, the relationship between pupil involvement and achievement may be positive, but it is variable, ranging from correlations of 0.1 to 0.6. Bennett notes that classroom observation suggests that the issue is more complex than time spent at work. What needs to be taken into account is the quality of that time, which is maximised by appropriate match of child to the learning experience, achieved by careful task setting.

Interestingly Bennett *et al.* (1984) explained that teachers tended to be unaware of the mismatch observed by the research team because of various processes of negotiation at work. Teachers tended to praise children for following procedure rather than for outcome or understanding, and tended not to focus on the more complex processes leading to task completion. Children politely worked on tasks that did not challenge while low attainers often spent much of their time waiting in queues for teacher attention.

This finding is corroborated in a US review (Doyle 1986) which noted that achieving students spent twice as much time on task as low-achieving pupils and completed three times as much work. While it might appear obvious that time on task is related to achievement, the relationship is far from simple in classrooms, as children can be taken off task because of their need for guidance.[2] West and Wheldall (1989) observed children waiting for teacher attention in 20 infant school classrooms and found that although the average waiting time was 84 seconds, in a quarter of the classrooms waiting time could exceed ten minutes and children were also observed to 'give up' waiting. West and Wheldall found that operating a mobile queue system was more effective than expecting children to sit in their places and raise their hands but they stress the need for further research in this area.

While West and Wheldall do not examine the reasons for demands for teacher attention, it would be fairly safe to assume that 'the queue' is made up of those children who need direct help and those who require teacher attention perhaps for procedural checks in mathematics, or spelling in language activities. As a result the less able are more likely to spend more time off task. Ways of dealing with demands on teacher time will be discussed later in this chapter.

It appears that pupil 'busyness' on task and teacher planning of pupil tasks are central classroom control issues. Nevertheless it is important to note that activity on task cannot always be equated with children's learning as quite complex processes of negotiation also centre around pupil performance on task and teacher task setting.

Negotiation

Flexible yet goal-oriented negotiation is an essential management skill. Within classrooms this skill helps to explain how tasks are implemented by teachers and interpreted by pupils in ways which ensure that order is maintained. While surveillance and 'busyness' explain classroom order in terms of control features, examination of negotiations allows exploration of the processes underpinning the management of learning.

Children are inducted into the rules and rituals of classroom life at the start of each academic year. Willes (1981) has documented this as a subtle use of teacher expectation in her study of reception classes. Teachers, she observed, tended to act as if the children understood the rules and so gradually brought children to an understanding of the social responsibilities inherent in being a pupil. Her study highlights the importance of the children's prior ability to interact with adults. There may well be specific difficulties for children from cultures or sub-cultures which do not share the social cues of the more dominant social groupings, the concerns of which are reflected in the processes of schooling.

Once the rules of 'being a pupil' have been accepted as the framework for pupil behaviour, a more focused form of negotiation appears to occur around classroom tasks. Here the observations of Doyle discussed in Chapters 4 and 5 are particularly helpful as they clearly relate classroom order to pupil learning (see Doyle, 1986, for an overview). As we have already outlined, he argues that tasks which are challenging to pupils because they demand a demonstration of understanding of topics, and because this may be open-ended in nature, are perceived as ambiguous by pupils. As a result children try to limit the riskiness of the demands by requesting more information and so lessen the cognitive challenge of the task. If pupils demand less ambiguity and fail to achieve it by successful negotiation with the teacher they may react with disruptive behaviour in order to avoid the task by other means. The success of pupils in negotiating down the level of task demand and the importance of keeping order sometimes leads experienced teachers to decide to omit more challenging tasks from their repertoire and so limit the learning experiences available to their pupils by concentrating, as Bennett *et al.* (1984) noted, on the procedural rather than the more cognitively challenging aspects of tasks.

These observations of the negotiation processes may not square either with the description of schooling as cultural transmission through the curriculum, or with the interactive model of learning presented in Chapter 5. There is obviously a need for the teacher to resolve the tensions and to ensure that children's learning of the curriculum is optimised.[3]

One method may simply lie in clearer goal setting for more risky or open-ended tasks. In their examination of learning strategies Nisbet and Shucksmith (1986) suggest that the clear explanation of goals to pupils is a prerequisite to pupil use of effective learning strategies as pupils are then able to assess and select ways of achieving these goals. Here the pedagogic emphasis is shifted from products to processes, pupil self-evaluation is encouraged and the risk of failing to achieve the correct solution is minimised.

Behavioural approaches in teaching

Another angle on classroom management can be seen in the Behavioural Approach to Teaching Package (BATPACK) developed by Wheldall and Merrett (1984, 1985). Their work aims to induct primary teachers into what they describe as 'positive' responses to children's behaviour through a school based in-service training programme. The focus is on classroom management and teachers are taught to examine the antecedents to pupil behaviour and, by selecting appropriate behavioural responses themselves, to provide positive reinforcement or encouragement for specifically defined pupil behaviours.

An enormous amount or research on behavioural approaches to teaching has been carried out in North America, and they have also had considerable influence in Britain. Their theoretical underpinning is in learning theory, and in the assumption that the same principles govern the 'learning' of behaviour as of any other task. Thus, if children enjoy receiving their teacher's attention, the teacher can use attention selectively as a way of increasing the frequency of particular behaviours. The behaviour may be writing a diary, working on the class project or sitting down except when invited to move around the classroom: the same reinforcement principles apply.[4]

Educational psychologists often provide 'behavioural', or 'behaviour modification' programmes to help teachers cope with difficult or disruptive behaviour. Typically, such programmes have six stages (see Table 6.1). The evidence for the effectiveness of behavioural approaches is contentious (see Berger, 1982). On the other hand, evaluations of BATPACK have reported changes in teacher behaviour, with evidence that positive reinforcement of appropriate pupil behaviour does help teachers in managing pupils, at least in the short to medium term.

Table 6.1 **Stages of a typical behavioural programme**

1.	Teacher identifies behaviour or skill which he/she wishes the class or a particular child to acquire, (or, in the case of behaviour, to modify).
2.	Obtain 'base-line' against which to measure subsequent progress. This is done by recording the frequency of the target behaviour.
3.	Analyse antecedents, or events which precede the target behaviour, and consequences, or events which follow it. This should show what is acting as a stimulus and/or as a reinforcement for the target behaviour.
4.	Using reinforcement principles, plan a programme to achieve the desired objective.
5.	Put the programme into practice, maintaining records so as to evaluate progress against the base-line measures.
6.	After reviewing progress, modify or develop the programme as necessary.

Nevertheless, two cautionary points should be made about the use of behavioural approaches. First, Wheldall (1982) has warned against 'behavioural overload', or the use of unnecessarily 'heavy', and perhaps primitive techniques to deal with relatively minor problems. In a similar vein, Berger (1979) warned of the danger of a 'mindless technology', and in a later article argued that 'classroom problems are influenced by a complex set of factors interacting and changing over time', and not simply by 'the behaviour of teachers or peers' (Berger, 1982, p. 292).

Wheldall's could be regarded as essentially technical points, resulting from inappropriate use of behavioural principles. Berger's point is more complex and challenges one of the behaviourists' most fundamental assumptions. This is that effective teaching depends on clear and precise specification of objectives. It is difficult to imagine teaching successfully without having clear objectives. Yet admitting that objectives are necessary to effective teaching does not mean that they are sufficient. McNamara (1988) has identified seven standard objections to an over-reliance on objectives (see also Eisner, 1985).

1. The rationale for selecting objectives is often unclear.
2. The detail with which objectives can be specified varies unacceptably from subject to subject: what precise objective must be met on the path to producing a creative, original story?
3. Splitting a curricular task into objectives can trivialise it: 'when we move on to pupils deploying their analytical and critical skills we simply cannot talk in terms of objectives' (McNamara, 1988, p. 41).
4. Specifying objectives generates either too few or too many. Unless the number is kept artificially low, children will learn far more in the course of a week than the teacher can specify as behavioural objectives.
5. The more varied and stimulating the curricular activities, the more difficult it becomes to obtain agreement on whether objectives have been achieved.
6. Whatever and however we teach, we convey attitudes through the hidden curriculum: 'The hidden curriculum which is associated with the objectives approach seems to have little to commend it.' (p. 42).
7. In however much detail objectives are specified, we still have to face questions about *how* we achieve them.

This said, it remains true that appropriateness of reinforcement is necessary for effective classroom management. Children are unlikely to respond well to teachers who appear uninterested in their efforts and unresponsive to their interests. Most teachers use reinforcement principles intuitively, but the evidence suggests that this is more frequently directed at appropriate educational tasks than at appropriate behaviour (Merrett and Wheldall, 1986). In other words, teachers seem to have difficulty in reinforcing 'good' behaviour, and may inadvertently encourage disruptive behaviours by directing their attention to the children concerned.

Classroom management and pupil learning

At a more general level it may be that the tension between cognitive challenge and classroom disorder may best be resolved through a greater emphasis on strategic planning, as disorder needs to be prevented rather than cured. From this it follows that the negotiation system should be sustained as breakdown would lead to disorder. The teacher's management role becomes one of creating operating systems for classroom groups which are clearly related to pupil task demands. Classroom rules need to be directed to the support of pupils who are engaged in learning activities. Put more simply, the needs of pupils while on task and while changing task need to be anticipated in the organisation and resourcing of the classroom. Classrooms need to be structured and rules agreed so that the support of pupils' active engagement on tasks over a maximum period of time, is the central issue. At a practical level this may mean, as examples, eliminating from the 'queue' those children who need to move on to the next task or to have access to a piece of equipment or careful resourcing of a problem-solving task. Again Doyle's (1986) analysis of classroom life is particularly helpful as it places an emphasis on the relationship between pupil learning and classroom management. This is because a coherent management system needs to be underpinned by a particular set of beliefs about what pupils need to learn and about how they best learn. The focus on pupil engagement on task, and on interaction with resources and teachers, allows us to recognise the relevance of his observations to the view of pupil learning described in Chapter 5.

Clearly there is more to classroom management than preventing chaos. Children attend school in order to learn. A system of classroom management which takes the learning needs of pupils as its starting point has clear advantages over one which is overly influenced by, for example, school traditions. The levels of task demand noted by Norman (1978) and outlined in Chapter 5, provide a useful link to relate pupils' learning needs to resourcing and use of teacher time. This link ensures that management issues spring from the assessment of pupils, an understanding of how pupils learn and a structured view of the relationship between tasks and the curriculum.

Using such a framework, planning of sessions starts with an assessment of learning needs of groups of pupils based upon their previous performances. These needs may be categorised according to the amount of teacher time they demand, for example introducing new ideas, monitoring children as they start to make sense, working on their own or resourcing their independent activity or practice tasks. Each type of activity demands specific resourcing and a varying amount of teacher time. The introduction of a new skill demands considerable pupil–teacher interaction; making sense of new knowledge and trying out an existing skill may only need careful resourcing and teacher monitoring while practice tasks may require careful prior resourcing but minimal teacher class time and much pupil self-direction. The relationship between the elements of children's learning, task, and teacher time can be seen in the lesson plan shown in Table 6.2.

Groups and grouping

The model we have just outlined is based on the assumption that teachers organise children into groups. Mortimore, *et al.* (1988) in their extensive study of London primary schools observed that 70 per cent of teachers made 'some use' of groups. Particularly within the basic subject areas of mathematics and language these groupings tended to be based on ability. However, these findings need to be interpreted with some caution. Over the three years of observations in junior schools, Mortimore and his team observed that most teacher communication occurred with individual pupils, followed by whole class interaction and finally by communication with groups, and that pupils worked alone for 68 per cent of the time that they were observed. As we noted in Chapter 4, interactive group work does not seem to be a feature of British classrooms, despite the popularity of grouping as an organisational strategy (e.g. see Bennett, 1985 and Yeomans, 1983 for overviews of research in this area).

Neither does grouping necessarily imply the implementation of an 'integrated day' in which several curriculum areas are in operation in one classroom at the same time. Mortimore *et al.* (1988) found that three-quarters of their observations occurred in classes which had a single subject focus.

From studies carried out in the United States, Doyle (1986) notes that the teacher is less likely to be at the centre of classroom organisation and instruction when various simultaneous activities occur and that student involvement tends to be lower in task areas in which the teacher is not involved. The latter observation is supported by Bennett (1985a) who cites a series of studies (e.g. Fisher *et al.*, 1978) to show the positive relationship between teacher supervision and pupil involvement with task in groups. In a similar vein Croll and Moses (1988) report a study of 32 junior classrooms which showed that

Table 6.2 *Lesson plan showing use of teacher time*

Date: . . . .   Session: . . . .

Children	Learning needs	Task	Resources	Teacher time
G				
R				
O Jenny	*Introduce*	*Discuss*	Rulers,	High
U Peter	measuring with	units of	pencil,	
P Ahmed	a ruler.	measurement.	papers,	
Winston	*Make sense*	*Measure*	as above	Medium
O Sarah	measuring	objects in	+ worksheets.	
N	with a ruler.	classroom.		
E				
G Andrea	*Practice*	*Workcards*	Workcards,	Low
R Paul	measuring in	on	series 2,	
O Siân	cms.	measurement.	cards 4–7,	
U Mehmet	*Introduce*	*Discuss*	cubes/boxes	High
P Jason	cubes.	shapes,	worksheets	
Karen		size,	pencils,	
T	*Make sense*	*Measure*	rulers	Medium
W	measuring sides.	cubes.		
O				
G				
R				
O	*Make Sense*			
U Cindy	planmaking	Continue	Graph paper,	Medium
P Patrick	3D shapes	with task	pencils,	
Charlie	etc.	from	rulers,	
T Tasha		yesterday.	scissors,	
H Jane			empty cartons.	
R	box making			
E				
E				

classrooms which had higher levels of whole-class interaction have higher levels of pupil time on task and that this higher engagement on task is evident during periods of individual activity as well as during class lessons. Clearly teachers appear to find management of both children and learning easier to handle in single subject sessions in the basic subjects at least. However, whether this is due to lack of experience and confidence in working an integrated day must still be open to question. Earlier in this chapter we noted that pedagogy is frequently shaped by resources and other situational constraints. Timetabling of space and whole-school activities may place just such a constraint on the effective development of curriculum integration. As a counterblast, the demands of a national curriculum may well only be met by an exploration of the ease and value of curriculum integration.

This is because cross-curricular planning may be the best way of dealing with the pressures of allocating specific proportions of the timetable to specified subject areas. While covering the entire curriculum through topic work may be neither desirable nor workable the topic approach may provide some practitioners with ways of covering overlapping areas of subject-specific targets or objectives. The planning of topic work necessarily becomes relatively rigid when operating to this rationale, but the method serves the dual purpose of covering a range of attainment targets and hopefully motivating children in a way familiar to expert practioners. (See ASE, 1989, for a useful guide to topic planning and the National Curriculum.)

Practical implications

The management of time

The aim here is to ensure optimal instructional contact with pupils. High quality interactions with pupils relate more to pupil thinking and learning than to the management of resources or task maintenance. Thinking of task demands in the way we have outlined in Table 6.3 may help focus the planning of instructional input.

Equally, the quality of pupils' use of time merits continuous review. Time on task may be a useful starting point, leading to a consideration of ways in which time is wasted (e.g. by waiting for teacher attention), but is a relatively low-level measure of pupil involvement when compared with the importance of the quality of the experience. Here management issues connect squarely with pupil learning around the notion of appropriate match of task and child.

No clear and simple guidelines for ensuring effective use of teacher time can be given as each classroom and series of tasks may demand a variety of strategies. The first step is to recognise the importance of time management and to review how time is spent. Once more we return to the Action Research methods of self-review mentioned in Chapter 1 in order to provide baseline data on which decisions for improved time management may be made. It may be helpful to keep an informal diary for a day or so to consider time use, or a simple checklist of questions may be more appropriate (see Fig 6.3).

Each teacher's individual profile would provide starting points for further action. This action might be the implementation of review sessions for the whole class to feedback, evaluate and set standards of work. A result of this could be to eliminate from the queue some of the pupils who constantly seem to want approval from the teacher. Other examples might be the shifting of more responsibility for equipment to the children or the end of marking alongside the child.

Within the framework of the interactive style of pedagogy we advocate it is difficult to separate use of teacher time from pupil time. Again the emphasis is on quality. Clear goal setting to reduce a fear of risk-taking complements an emphasis on process goals, e.g. planning, selecting and evaluating. The matching of task and child is pivotal and has been discussed in Chapter 5, but careful assessment of pupil performance on task necessarily underpins future task setting and is more likely to ensure a higher quality engagement on task. At a very practical level, when pupils feel that they 'own' the classroom's learning resources, when they have a clear idea of how much work is expected in each session, their autonomy is increased and many of the more mundane demands on teacher attention are removed. This allows more opportunity for the teacher to focus on children's thinking and learning. Management of time is therefore explicitly related to the management of space and the management of materials.

Table 6.3 **A 'use of time' teacher prompt list**

Interactions with other adults	
–	Head teacher
–	Other colleagues
–	Parents
–	Domestic staff
–	Others

Domestic chores undertaken

e.g.	Sweeping up sand
	Giving out equipment

Main activities with children

List:

The management of space

As we have already observed the management of space both determines and is determined by pedagogical priorities. If the decisions of the teacher are to be led by a set of beliefs in how children best think and learn, positive planning of the available space would seem essential.

An interactional pedagogy which contains within it elements of surveillance, activity (or 'busyness') and negotiation would suggest that the teacher needs to be near to as many pupils as possible for as much of the time as possible. The traditional notion of a desk-bound teacher is rarely observed, yet remnants of that model may still exist in the positioning of the teacher's base and pupil work areas. Nevertheless, maximal contact between pupils and teachers implies the opportunity for whole-class teaching and review, working with groups and monitoring of pupils.

Carpeted corners for whole-class sessions are now commonplace, afford optimum opportunity for pupil–teacher contact and can double as reading and activity corners. Less evident is an awareness of how important it is for the teacher as 'ringmaster', to place him or herself centrally and so avoid problems such as being trapped against a wall with a group needing instruction, while at the other side of the room children are wandering off task for lack of a monitorial check from the teacher. Placing work tables against walls and windows may lose less space at the table than might be imagined and may help create a cleared central area in which the teacher can operate as instructor and monitor to a maximum number of pupils.

Other consequences of positioning work tables peripherally may be the release of display areas which had previously been hidden by high-backed storage units. These units would consequently have to be deployed more centrally, perhaps to increase the number of work areas or 'corners' available for the more pupil directed 'making sense' or 'practice' activities.

Again no clear guidelines can be given as not all classrooms are equipped with tables or mobile storage units. Once more it is a question of self-review and a questioning of the match between pedagogical beliefs and the use of resources available.

The management of materials

Our emphasis on the quality of the interaction between teacher and pupil suggests the need to consider the content of interactions with children. Tizard and Hughes (1984) reported that 70 per cent of questions asked by the working-class pre-school girls while at school were routine business questions. This was not the case for the middle-class girls for whom 36 per cent of questions were business. However, both proportions suggest the need to address this issue.

Given that time in classrooms is organised by teachers in terms of tasks for children, the resourcing of these activities requires detailed attention. Careful prior resourcing limits options available to the learner helping to ensure that the child does face challenges and can avoid easier, already well-practised, solutions. Equally, careful preparation of materials releases the teacher for work with pupils while they are on task and helps eliminate the more mundane questions relating to starting tasks. Within the model of lesson planning provided earlier in this chapter, careful resourcing of pupils' experiences would be considered crucial to the second or 'making sense' level of the learning experience. The absentee teacher is still very much in control of the pupils' curricular activities, yet able to focus his or her interactions on the immediate learning needs of other pupils.

Another consequence of the high value to be placed on teacher time is the need to consider ways in which the classroom may become self-running. Methods include giving specific responsibilities to individual pupils and training all pupils in group responsibilities. However, in terms of materials it necessitates ensuring the accessibility of resources and instructions for tasks. Yet again each professional needs to consider each situation: for example, how much time is wasted asking permission to use scissors or waiting to have paper cut? What kind of follow-up 'making sense' or practice activities could be written out on work cards and kept in a small box on an activity table for that odd five or ten minutes for early finishers?

Giving children the right to use materials with the consequent responsibility for their final selection and, within a clear framework, to select tasks, may be an important step forward in freeing the teacher to act as professional pedagogue. Classroom management strategies can only be justified by their capacity to facilitate pupils' learning.

Notes and further reading

1. A clear account of teaching styles and pupil organisation in primary schools can be found in the results of the ORACLE project of the late 1970s, e.g. Galton, M., Simon, B. and Croll, P. (1980) *Inside the Primary Classroom*. London, Routledge and Kegan Paul.

    From a sociological perspective, Sharp and Green (1975) provide a discursive analysis of progressive tactics and social control in primary schools. (Sharp R., and Green A.G., (1975) *Education and Social Control*. London, Routledge and Kegan Paul.)

    Walkerdine (1984) moves beyond some of the points raised by Sharp and Green to examine ways in which specific forms of developmental psychology have sustained a set of classroom practices in primary schools. (Walkerdine, V. (1984) Developmental Psychology and the Child-centred Pedagogy. In J. Henriques, W. Hollway, C. Urwin, C. Venn and V. Walkerdine. *Changing the Subject*. London, Methuen.)

2. A good introduction to the topic of time on task is Bennett, N. (1985b) Time to teach: teaching-learning processes in Primary School. In N.J. Entwistle (ed.) *New Directions in Educational Psychology – Learning and Teaching*. Lewes, Falmer Press.

    The ORACLE studies also examined time on task. Brief references to the topic can be found in the following two volumes:
    Galton, M. and Simon, B. (eds) (1980) *Progress and Performance in the Primary Classroom*. London, Routledge and Kegan Paul.
    Galton, M. and Willcocks, J. (eds) (1983) *Moving from the Primary Classroom*. London, Routledge and Kegan Paul.

    More detailed information can be found in Anderson, L.W. (ed.) (1986) *Time and School Learning*. London, Croom Helm.

3. Ways in which control is negotiated in classrooms have been a research focus in the sociology of education over the last two decades. Interesting papers can be found in the following collections:

Woods, P. and Hammersley, M. (eds.) (1977) *School Experience*. London, Croom Helm.

Woods, P. (ed.) (1980a) *Pupil Strategies*. London, Croom Helm.

Woods, P. (ed.) (1980b) *Teacher Strategies*. London, Croom Helm.

4.   Useful introductions to the use of applied behaviour analysis in the classroom are:

Harrop A., (1983) *Behaviour Modification in the Classroom*. London, Hodder and Stoughton.

Wheldall K., and Glynn T., (1989) *Effective Classroom Learning*. Oxford, Blackwell.

A reader containing many of the seminal articles on classroom behaviour modification is:

O'Leary, K.D. and S.C., (1979) *Classroom Management: the Successful Use of Behaviour Modification in the Classroom* (2nd edn.). New York, Pergamon.

Suggestions for seminar activities

1.   Ask students to consider their current classroom, or one in which they have recently worked. Ask them to draw a plan of the classroom, placing furniture, display areas as they currently stand. As a first stage activity students can discuss, in pairs, the rationale or justification for existing use of space. Points to be considered could include the importance of surveillance, busyness and negotiation. Remaining in the same pairings, a second stage activity could involve students in examining ways in which the layout might be changed in the light of some of the points raised by this chapter.

2.   Prior to the seminar ask each student to monitor or observe one child for a period of up to twenty minutes, noting as much as possible of what she or he is doing on a minute by minute basis. A proforma might help, for example:

Time in minutes	Child's actions	Additional notes
11.01		
11.02		
11.03		

Ask students to analyse the information to consider how much time was spent engaged on task. Seminar discussion could focus on how that time might be increased and on the importance of the quality of the task and the level of engagement.

3.   Ask students to work alone to think of one 'typical' teaching day from the moment they arrive until they leave school at the end of the day. Ask them to list, in chronological order when possible, the activities a teacher undertakes, e.g. prepare resources (mix paints, cut paper, wash sponges), talk with parents, tell story, listen to 'news'. Ask them to work in pairs to categorise these activities. You may want to suggest your own categories, but the following may be useful starting points: 'could be delegated to

children', 'important for children's thinking and learning', 'important for children's social and emotional development', 'not a productive use of time'. Some activities may fall in several categories.

Discuss as a group (a) how teacher time might be used most productively and (b) how the less productive activities may be curtailed or delegated, perhaps to pupils as educationally valuable activities.

CHAPTER 7

Personal and social education

Introduction

After the Plowden Report (CACE, 1967) primary teachers sometimes used to claim that they taught children not subjects. With the nomination of teachers with designated responsibility in each curriculum area, not to mention the introduction of the National Curriculum, this claim is heard less often. Nevertheless, primary teachers still claim an interest in, and responsibility for, pupils' 'overall' development. Indeed any suggestion that primary schooling may sometimes be less than wholly beneficial to pupils' personal and social development is likely to be greeted with bewilderment or outrage: 'But you don't seem to understand: this is central to absolutely everything we do'.

Certainly, there can be few schools, if any, which do not claim a commitment to their pupils' well-being which extends beyond their progress in the National Curriculum. Nor can there be many which deny a fundamental commitment to personal and social education. Yet the meaning of personal and social education in terms of day-to-day classroom practice remains tantalisingly unclear. This chapter aims to unravel what may be meant by personal and social education and to consider its practical implications for primary school and classroom practice. We shall start by examining the concept of personal and social education and its aims, and will then consider some of the tensions to which they give rise. We shall then move to the curricular implications, and finally to the school's relationship with its pupils' parents, and the impact this may have on their development.

Concept and aims of personal and social education

The inevitability of personal and social education

Even if they wanted to, teachers could not avoid having an impact on pupils' personal and social development. Children develop as members of social groups: the family, extended family, playgroup, school and so on. As we have argued throughout the book, this involves a process of mutual adaptation. At school, children adapt to their teacher's expectations, either by behaving in the accepted way, or, occasionally otherwise. This adaptation process entails that they learn from the way the school is organised and from their teacher's response to different situations. They will learn about power relationships from the way they are treated, *and* from observation of interaction between the headteacher and other staff. They will certainly learn, for better or worse, what their teachers consider to be suitable behaviour, dress and activities for boys and for girls. Some of the most blatant examples of naively sexist expectations and requirements that we have observed have been in infant school. To illustrate the inevitability of personal and social education, consider three situations:

1. A reception class teacher sees Jamie on top of Janice in the Wendy house, in a fair simulation of the missionary position. They are, Jamie explains, playing mums and dads.
2. A junior school teacher hears a boy say: 'fuck it' as the class settles down at the start of the lesson. A month later the same teacher hears the same expletive from a girl, this time in the playground.
3. A fight starts in the mid-morning playtime. A Bangladeshi boy says that he has been called names, and that he's going to 'get' the name-callers. Further investigation reveals that the name calling is racist in nature.

We do not wish to consider here how the teacher should react to these incidents. Each of them, though, is likely to be familiar to experienced teachers. Our point is simply that children will learn *something* from the teacher's reaction, irrespective of what this reaction may be.

Defining personal and social education

Elsewhere David Galloway has defined personal and social education as all learning experiences from which pupils derive:

a developing sense of their own abilities and of their rights and responsibilities as contributing members of the school and of the wider community in which they live (Galloway, 1990, p. 10).

By a 'developing' sense of their rights and responsibilities we imply simply that pupils' concepts of themselves and of their position in their family, school and society develop with age. How the concept of self develops is the school's responsibility as well as the parents, though tension is likely when parents and teachers differ in their views of the school's role. Many of the learning experiences which affect pupils' personal and social development are incidental, arising from the school's hidden curriculum. We shall nevertheless argue that personal and social education has important implications for classroom management. It also has implications for the curriculum which requires careful planning as part of the National Curriculum. At this stage we need to look at issues arising from our definition of personal and social education and at some of the problems arising from it.[1]

Whose rights and responsibilities?

Logically, we cannot talk about children developing a sense of their rights and responsibilities as contributing members of the school without also considering our own rights and responsibilities as teachers. Asking what children, or their parents, should feel entitled to expect from school is perhaps one of the most effective ways of setting ourselves high standards. There is very little here that we can take for granted. If we consider seemingly straightforward expectations such as: 'children shouldn't be made to feel inferior by criticism', or 'children should feel they learn from their mistakes' we may find ourselves in deep water. Diener and Dweck (1978) have agreed that children develop 'learned helplessness' when they feel that teachers are criticising them as individuals, rather than criticising aspects of their performance on a specific task. Helping them to see why they are finding something difficult, whether it be learning to read or grasping a new concept in mathematics, is perhaps one of the most challenging tasks for a teacher. Too often children interpret what teachers say to them or write in their books ('critical feedback' in the jargon) as a comment on their own ability rather than as a way of helping them to master the task in hand. [2]

Values and beliefs

Whenever we state what standard we expect from pupils, for example, in dress or behaviour, we are influenced by our own values and beliefs. The problem here is that each teacher's own beliefs and values will certainly differ from those of many pupils and their parents.

Two examples of beliefs are: 'There is but one God, Allah', and 'Jesus is Lord'. Two examples of values are: 'We should respect the religious beliefs of others', and 'we should not make fun of people because they are disabled'. Differences in religious and political belief may be associated with differences in values. Most Quakers, for example, would argue that war is never morally justified. This is a value judgement, derived from their belief that the biblical injunction to turn the other cheek proscribes violence in any circumstances. Other Christian groups do not share this belief, and consequently adopt different values.

In spite of the interrelationship between values and beliefs, it remains true that no community can flourish without broad agreement on values. Lack of such agreement leads inevitably to anarchy. Any school or children's organisation requires a generally agreed, though not immutable, set of values in order to maintain a climate of stability in which learning is possible. It also requires some concept of its own interrelationship with wider groups. Yet as we have already argued, teachers are not free agents. Through successive Education Acts, the government is encouraging a particular set of values. In their visits of inspection, HMI take a keen interest in the school's philosophy and social climate. Parents may impose values on a school, for example commitment to uniformity of dress, by means of an implicit threat to send their children elsewhere. It follows that the values which the head and staff seek to promote throughout a school cannot be totally idiosyncratic. If they are rejected, or just not understood, by a majority of parents, no policy on personal and social education is likely to be effective. Another influence, which is still of some importance, is that of the LEA. Just as the teacher's values are reflected in the written and unwritten policies of the school, so the collective values of the Education Committee may also be formalised into a set of more or less well-defined policies which attempt to influence the values adopted and promoted by teachers.

Notable examples in recent years are anti-racism and anti-sexism policies. Some LEAs have requested each school to produce its own policy for combatting racism and sexism. It is important to note that the assumed need for a formal policy to combat these problems implies that the teachers' existing value systems may tolerate, or even foster, behaviour which discriminates against pupils or fellow staff members on the basis of race or sex. The success of an anti-racist or anti-sexist policy at LEA level in overcoming racist or sexist practices in schools remain a matter for research. What is not in doubt is that what pupils learn in school about personal relationships, with each other and with adults, will be influenced by their perception of their teachers' values. The clarity with which these are formulated and expressed will be reflected in the schools' climate and hidden curriculum.

The most far-reaching attempt to influence the values which schools seek to develop has not, however, come from LEAs but from central government in the form of the 1988 Education Act. The introduction of a national curriculum places an explicit value on an organised, and centrally determined body of knowledge, while national testing seeks to develop a competitive ethos within and between schools. The increase in parents' freedom to select their children's school, their greater representation on governing bodies and the local financial management of schools may all be seen as an attempt to increase a sense of parental and community responsibility for what happens in schools.

Tensions in personal and social education

Care and control: educational policy issues

No country could afford to be unconcerned about the impact of schooling on children's personal and social development. There is no system of government in which politicians could truthfully say: 'We have neither concern nor responsibility for the values, knowledge and skills that our children develop.' Education, then, can never be apolitical. The origins of compulsory state education in Britain are sometimes thought to lie in an altruistic concern for the plight of young children in the factories and mines and in the growing belief that education was intrinsically humanising and liberating. Sadly, the evidence to support this cosily benevolent view is rather limited. A more realistic appraisal sees the introduction of compulsory education for all as a way of socialising children into accepting their 'rightful' place in society by teaching them the values they would need as acceptable employees in late nineteenth and early twentieth-century industrial society.[3]

Both in democracies and in totalitarian states teachers are subject to pressure over both the official and the hidden curriculum. The nature and strength of the pressure varies widely, depending on whether those in power regard the current status quo as acceptable. In Britain a liberal view of education went largely unchallenged for some thirty years after the Second World War. This saw education as intrinsically desirable for it own sake with little reason to doubt that schools would produce young people with the attitudes and skills needed to play a useful part in society. The Plowden Report on primary education lent powerful support to this view with its commitment to child-centred learning and its belief in the school's contribution in mitigating the effects of social disadvantage.

The rhetoric of liberal education suited teachers since it allowed them extensive control over the curriculum. At a time of low unemployment and increasing prosperity it also suited successive governments. Sociologists and psychologists could draw attention to inequality within the education system, as well as within society, arguing for example, that it merely equipped 'working class kids for working class jobs' (Willis, 1977), but as long as most people had jobs and living standards continued to rise schools remained relatively free from political attention. The fact that over 12 per cent of pupils left school with no formal qualification (Fontana, 1984) was of little political importance.

James Callaghan signalled that all this was changing in a speech at Ruskin College in 1976, thereby unleashing a debate that led ultimately to the 1988 Education Reform Act. A combination of factors created increasing political interest in education. They included rising unemployment, the growing power of the unions, the decline of traditional industries with their demand for unskilled or semi-skilled labour, technological changes with consequent demand for new skills, and the growth of smaller industries requiring a more specialised and more adaptable work force. In this climate the traditional liberal curriculum appeared out-dated, posing a threat to the country's economic prosperity. More important, if large numbers of pupils continued to leave school with no marketable skills and no prospect of employment the stability of the country would be threatened. It was not enough, though, to introduce a national curriculum. At least as important, teachers had to expect more of children, and parents had to expect more of teachers. In educational jargon, the liberal view of education gave way to an instrumental one, in which schools and colleges were seen as an instrument for social change. The ethos of liberal education for some and learning to labour for others was replaced by the enterprise culture for all, at least in political rhetoric. The impact of an increasingly vocational orientation in the curriculum did not escape primary schools. Representatives from local industry and commerce were appointed to governing bodies. HMI started to take an interest in evidence of children's understanding of industry. Primary teacher training courses had to satisfy a government committee that students were being equipped to develop their future pupils' understanding of the world of work. (DES, 1989a).

Psychology and personal and social education

The political attention to education throughout the 1980s was explicitly motivated by interest in the personal qualities that schools should, according to the government, be developing in their pupils. This raises questions about the contribution that psychology makes to the theory and practice of personal and social education. It should by now be clear that psychology can never tell teachers what is 'appropriate' personal and social education, nor can it specify with any authority the aims or scope of personal and social education. Psychologists do claim to tell us what concepts children can grasp at different ages. This has obvious implications for understanding children's moral development, though even here there is controversy between different schools of thought. Returning to our definition of personal and social education, psychology cannot tell us what are appropriate rights and responsibilities for children of different ages since these are culturally or politically determined. The Conservative government of the 1980s appeared to see the function of personal and social education as preparing young people to take their place as responsible citizens and employees (e.g. DES, 1985). This does not always rest comfortably with the more liberal tradition of creating questioning, critical, autonomous young people who think and act for themselves, willing 'to resist exploitation, to innovate and to be vigilant in the defence of liberty', as was recognised in a joint DES/HMI document in 1977. It is worth noting that the concept of personal and social education is politically as well as psychologically and morally neutral. It was considered at least as important in Hitler's Germany as in any late twentieth-century Western democracy. Our point is that while different people may agree on the importance of personal and social education, they may have entirely different things in mind, depending on their political, moral and religious values.

Care and control: school and classroom policy

All social groups have rules to regulate the behaviour of their members. In primary schools a few rules are explicit, for example not leaving the playground in the lunch hour without permission. The majority, though, are implicit. Observation of classes in any primary school will reveal differences between teachers both in the behaviour and in the work they expect from children, the way they organise the start and finish of lessons and the organisation of the lesson itself. Rules, however, imply the possibility of rule-breaking. As we have indicated in Chapters 4 and 6, teachers naturally expect children to accept the rules they consider necessary for the safe and efficient running of the school. In this respect they are no different from leaders of any other social group. When children do not conform to the 'normal' expectations, teachers invoke sanctions, again like leaders of any other social group. These may include talking to the child, using peer pressure: 'we don't do this kind of thing', seating the child in a different place, sending him or her to the head teacher, or discussing the problem with parents. In broad terms, acceptance of a teacher's general expectations is seen as 'normal'. Children who continue to present serious behavioural problems may be seen as needing special 'help'. The same, incidentally, applies to children who fail to make the expected progress in the curriculum. A high proportion of children seen by educational psychologists are referred on account of behaviour problems, often in conjunction with learning difficulties.

This too raises questions about psychology's contribution to primary teaching. Psychologists can draw on research evidence on the 'normality' of different behaviour in purely statistical terms. Thus, they can tell parents what per cent of children are left-handed, and reassure them that this carries no implications for future educational problems. Similarly, they can reassure teachers that shy or withdrawn children are likely to improve, whereas, other problems such as truancy, stealing or bullying are more likely to persist. Unreassuringly again, an honest psychologist would have to add that both statements remain true irrespective of whether specialised help is provided.[4] Ultimately, however, psychologists have to make a value judgement on the significance of behaviour problems referred to them. This should entail considering the problem from the teacher's point of view as well as its relevance to the child's current and future development. Hence, teachers have a legitimate expectation that psychologists should be able to help them with problems of classroom management.

Few educational psychologists would quarrel with this expectation. They claim expertise in methods of behaviour change which have particular relevance to teachers. Yet behind the teacher's decision to seek specialised help and the psychologist's acceptance of the referral, lie assumptions about 'normal' personal and social development and 'normal' discipline. Thirty years ago many primary school children were expected to stand in silence when a visitor entered the classroom. Today that is blessedly rare except in the most formal independent schools. What constitutes 'normal' behaviour and normal discipline changes with popular and professional opinion. As important, different tasks in school demand different styles of behaviour (see Chapter 4). The methods which teachers and psychologists use to help/encourage/coerce children into acceptable behaviour also change. Thanks to the European Court of Human Rights, corporal punishment has finally been abolished in Britain. Similarly, some of the more extreme methods of behaviour modification, such as placing children in 'time-out' isolation rooms, have been quietly dropped. What remains constant is the link between the teacher's need for discipline and control on the one hand and assumptions about pupil's personal and social development on the other.

Classroom management and children's moral development

The need for rules is logically independent of the need for children to understand the reasons for them. Toddlers for example, are taught not to put their fingers into electric plug sockets without having any clear understanding of the precise reasons. Yet if we are committed to see children as active learners it is important that they should understand reasons for what teachers and parents expect of them, and recognise the consequences of not conforming to these expectations. If, then, we see children as actively involved in their own learning we cannot sensibly set standards of behaviour without reference to what they understand by right and wrong. Kohlberg (1975) has argued that this is related to their level of cognitive development. He proposed six stages of moral development (see Table 7.1) but suggested that many people never progress beyond stage four. Kohlberg's higher stages of moral reasoning imply the moral right to question the prevailing norms in a society, as reflected, for example, in national legislation or in school rules. Thus, rules can, and sometimes should, be challenged.

While Kohlberg's theory has been widely criticised,[5] it raises an interesting question about teachers' responses to 'difficult' behaviour. To what level of moral reasoning do the most frequently used responses apply. Infant school teachers usually rely on appeals to their own relationship with the children, together with insight into the effect of the action on other children: 'How do you think Jenny felt when you splashed her work with paint?' or 'How would you have felt if someone had done that to you?' This would correspond to stage three. Similarly, most junior school heads would deal with the occasional case of a child smoking by discussing the harmful and dependency forming effects of the habit, combined, perhaps, with informing the child's parents about the incident. This, too, would correspond to stage three.

In some schools, sanctions are more explicit, mainly with older pupils, perhaps involving a 'tariff' system: 'If you chatter in class time you stay in to finish your work at play-time', or 'if you talk in assembly you spend 20 minutes of your lunch hour picking up litter'.

Table 7.1 **Kohlberg's theory of moral reasoning**

Level 1	(Corresponds to Piaget's 'preconventional' stage: approximate age 2–7.)
Stage 1:	Obedience/conformity due solely to fear of punishment. *Example:* You mustn't talk when the teacher tells you to be quiet because you might get told off.
Stage 2:	Morality based on 'fair trades'. *Example:* You must share your toys with other children so that they will share theirs with you.
Level 2	(Corresponds to Piaget's 'conventional' stage: approximate 7–11.)
Stage 3:	Judgement based on desire to please others. *Example:* It's wrong to swear because it upsets mum (teacher).
Stage 4:	Judgement based on respect for authority, maintaining law and order. *Example:* You mustn't break rules even if you don't agree with them. What would happen if everyone decided on rules for themselves?
Level 3	(Corresponds to Piaget's 'post-conventional' stages: age 12 upwards.)
Stage 5:	Rules can be changed if there is general agreement. *Example:* Why is this rule really necessary?
Stage 6:	Respect for human dignity: abstract principles can transcend rules. *Example:* I won't obey this rule because it's against my principles.

Tariff systems of this kind appeal to the lowest level of moral reasoning, and are really more appropriate for preschool children (provided the connection between the act and the response is immediate). They can have a deterrent value too. Yet from the point of view of personal and social development they are at best useless. They do little to develop respect for the moral legitimacy of rules nor, incidentally, do they give teachers any incentive for questioning the necessity for a rule. Rather they encourage deviousness by instilling respect for the eleventh commandment: 'Thou shalt not be found out.'

Personal and social education and the curriculum

Both the official, or National Curriculum, and the hidden curriculum contribute to children's personal and social education. The hidden curriculum can be defined as the network of relations in a school, between teachers, between pupils and between teachers and pupils which determine what teachers and pupils expect of themselves and of each other. Both pupils' and teachers' expectations are influenced by the structure of the society in which they live. Authors with a Marxist orientation tend to regard the social and economic divisions in society as having an overwhelming influence on the hidden curriculum (e.g. Bowles and Gintis, 1976). This deterministic view underestimates the ability both of teachers and pupils to take independent action in protection of their interests.[6] Nevertheless it is difficult to underestimate the importance of the hidden curriculum. It includes all incidental learning and reflects the social and emotional climate of the school. Many sociologists see it as one of the most powerful means by which society defines the value attached to different kinds and levels of achievement, and thereby shapes the future behaviour of its citizens.

The National Curriculum may contain messages that are transmitted through the hidden curriculum. Thus, more time is allocated to Maths than to Music, to Science than to Physical Education. Additional influences in the hidden curriculum lie in the organisation of the class, the school and the education system itself. We have already referred to the 'lessons' children learn about sex roles from the organisation of infant and junior school classes. Relationships between senior and main professional grade staff are a further influence. The existence of the private sector draws explicit attention to the power of money to buy what many parents see as educational privilege. For parents and for children it is a short step from believing that education at the local primary is unsatisfactory to concluding that the children who attend it are less desirable as friends. City technology colleges and grant maintained schools may produce the same divisiveness within the state system as already exists between state and independent schools.

Personal and social education does not form part of the National Curriculum. On the other hand teachers' conditions of service explicitly require them to communicate and consult with parents and outside bodies, take part in meetings about pastoral arrangements and promote 'the general progress and well-being of individual pupils and of any class or group of pupils' assigned to them (DES, 1988a, p. 23). In addition the National Curriculum Council has set up a working party in which personal and social education is seen as one of a number of cross-curricular themes. (National Curriculum Council, 1989).

The status of personal and social education in the primary curriculum is, in fact, highly problematic. If we accept that some of the most powerful influences on children's personal and social development are transmitted through the hidden curriculum it is nonsensical to argue that personal and social education should be identified as a specific area of the national curriculum. Theoretically, it would be nice to think that *everything* that happens in schools, both through the national and through the hidden curriculum contributes beneficially to children's personal and social development. Regrettably, there appear to be good reasons for doubting that we have yet reached this happy state of affairs. Regarding the whole area as unproblematic prevents a clear analysis of ways in which schools affect their pupils' personal and social development.

A starting point is to identify themes and issues of particular relevance. Curricular themes could include health and sex education, a developing understanding of the world of work, awareness of the neighbourhood around the school, world affairs, the organisation of society and so on. Some of them sound rather abstract for 6 year-olds, but these children can surely start to appreciate why they stay at home on election day when the school becomes a polling station. Issues which require specific attention could include gender, race, rights and responsibilities, awareness of risks and how to say no.

Planning the personal and social education curriculum

The range and complexity of the themes and issues identified above indicates the need for a planned programme of personal and social education. As well as developing a clear school policy on equal opportunities with respect to gender and race, teachers have to agree on the aspects of each theme which should be covered in each year group. A policy for the whole school is necessary for two reasons. The first is the traditional autonomy of the primary class teacher. The second is the prominent place in the primary curriculum of project and topic work. A programme for each year group is needed: (a) to avoid omitting issues which teachers and governors consider important; (b) to avoid duplication; some issues will be repeated in consecutive years, but not at the same level; (c) to ensure a broad consensus on what the school is trying to achieve with respect to personal and social education. This implies the need for a school programme on personal and social education, just as for Mathematics, English, Science and other subjects in the National Curriculum. The question is who should be responsible for planning this.

Three principles appear important. First, to ensure coherence and development across the age-range, the head or an experienced nominee will need to convene a small group of teachers to produce the outline programme referred to earlier. This will identify issues which should be covered, and at what stage in the year. In other words the personal and social education programme will provide clear guidelines on what should be covered, but will not override the class teacher's autonomy by undermining the flexibility which characterises good primary teaching, allowing the teacher to incorporate a wide range of curriculum experiences into work on a project or on a particular theme. Third, the fact that class teachers retain this autonomy implies the need for guidance and support from an experienced colleague. Under the teachers' new conditions of service (DES, 1988a), all teachers may be expected to develop an area of specific expertise. Given its complexity, it seems logical that one teacher should be given responsibility for developing expertise in personal and social education. A major purpose in requiring all teachers to develop an area of specific expertise is, of course, to facilitate and extend school-based INSET. This does not mean that the main task of the teacher involved in personal and social education will be to provide sessions for the whole staff on INSET days, though this may be desirable from time to time. It *does* mean that he or she will be available on a day-to-day basis for discussion with colleagues on ways to incorporate aspects of the year's personal and social education programme into the projects or themes on which children are currently working.

All this raises questions about assessment. Superficially, this can be carried out by monitoring the knowledge, skills, attitudes and concepts which children acquire or develop from their school's personal and social education programme. Yet assessment of children's personal and social development has to go much further than this, requiring a broader picture of their overall development. That, however, is only possible in terms of the school's aims for its pupils' personal and social development. This brings us back to the qualities that teachers, parents, school governors, the LEA and central government believe children should be developing at school. To say these are essentially political value judgements, and therefore not part of a teacher's job, is an evasion of responsibility. The fact that a school is part of a wider community does not mean teachers can avoid a clear statement of their own position on basic moral issues. A community with no values is an amoral one. If we are clear about the moral and social aims of schooling, we shall wish to develop ways of monitoring pupils' development that extend beyond their progress in subjects of the National Curriculum.

Personal and social education and parents

Teachers vary widely in their beliefs and values. Indeed the sheer variety of their beliefs and values is one of the most powerful arguments for developing an agreed policy on the values the school seeks to develop in pupils. Parents are likely to differ even more widely, if only because there are more of them. Successive Education Acts have shifted the balance of power between teachers and parents in the latter's favour. The 1980 Act required secondary schools to publish public examination results. It also required the publication of HMI reports on schools, gave parents access to greater information about a school's organisation and curriculum, and extended their rights to choose their child's school. The 1981 Act gave parents extensive rights to involvement in the assessment of their child's special educational needs, including copies of professional reports. The 1986 Act ensured their representation on all governing bodies. The 1988 Act gave them the National Curriculum, the promise of information on their children's performance in the proposed national testing programme, the possibility of opting out of LEA control by seeking grant-maintained status, and a further increase in choice of their child's school.

There is little doubt that part of the motivation behind all this legislation was the government's view that schools had been insufficiently responsive to parents' aspirations and unreasonably secretive both in their control of the curriculum and in their communication with parents. Nor is there much doubt that schools in Britain compare unfavourably with those in other EEC countries in terms of the quality of cooperation between home and school (Macbeth, 1984). A deeply entrenched part of staff-room folklore in many schools, especially those serving council housing estates, inner-city areas and areas with many pupils from minority ethnic communities is that parental 'apathy' is widespread.

The evidence does not support this view. Numerous studies of parental interest in their children's education have demonstrated that parents are much more actively interested than is accepted by the conventional wisdom in many staff-rooms (e.g. Johnson and Ranson, 1983). In addition, a one-sidedness is evident in a lot of 'liaison' with parents (see Woods, 1988; Johnson and Ranson, 1983). Teachers often see their task as educating parents about the school rather than as understanding the parents' own values and priorities. Cooperative parents, then, are ones who do not rock the boat, content to support the school even when a more objective view might suggest that their child's curricular or social needs are not adequately being met.

Making schools parent-friendly

How much the individual class or subject teacher can do to foster an effective partnership with parents will depend to some extent on the school's senior management. They can make the school 'parent friendly', or provide hidden messages that deter parents even more effectively than a printed notice saying: No Parents Beyond This Point. In this section we consider how class teachers can contribute to the school's overall policy.

Parents are more likely to believe teachers' protestations about their importance in their children's education if these are accompanied by practical suggestions. Hewison and Tizard (1980) provided a fascinating example.

Parents were asked to listen to their infant-age children reading from books they brought home from school. A subsequent study showed that parental listening produced greater gains than provision of extra reading lessons at school from an experienced teacher (Tizard *et al.*, 1982). Parents were *not* given elaborate guidance on *how* to listen to their children. More important, the research took place in schools with a multi-ethnic intake in Haringey, a socially disadvantaged part of London. This was precisely the sort of area in which parents would be least likely, according to conventional wisdom, to be able and willing to help in their children's education.

The Haringey research has been confirmed elsewhere (e.g. Widlake and Macleod, 1984) and Young and Tyre (1983) also found benefits for children with specific reading difficulties when their parents listened to their reading. This is a group which is generally thought to need very specialised help. An interesting feature of the Haringey research was that the children's reading improved even if the parents did not understand English. It is not clear how parental involvement in the curriculum may improve children's progress, but elsewhere I have suggested four possibilities (Galloway, 1987).

1. It is well known that skills learned in one context do not necessarily transfer to another. By listening to their children reading from books they bring home from school, parents help to overcome problems of learning transfer.
2. By listening to their children reading parents demonstrate the importance they attach to their progress at school and thus increase their motivation to succeed at school.
3. Arising from the last point, parents who are themselves illiterate often value literacy extremely highly: friendly encouragement to cooperate with the school is encouraged and leads parents and children to view school attendance in a different light.
4. Establishing cooperative contact with parents and observing the beneficial results on children's progress is likely to change teachers' perceptions of their pupils' parents. . . Children are

sensitive to their teacher's attitudes. A sense that their parents and teachers are working together seems likely to contribute to a climate of security favourable to successful learning (pp. 180–1).

So far we have been taking about parent's involvement at home in the teaching of their children to read. It is not difficult to think of similar opportunities in other areas of the curriculum or in other age-groups. More difficult is provision of opportunities for parents to help in the classroom. This happens in many infant classes, fewer junior classes and scarcely at all in secondary schools. The reasons are not hard to see. The curriculum for older children tends to be more teacher-led. The children themselves may be less dependent on adult help, and they may resent or be embarrassed by the presence of their parents. Providing opportunities for parents to contribute to mainstream school activities can nevertheless be fruitful. Open days on which parents are welcome to sit in on any class is a more artificial but still potentially useful exercise.

Teachers' conditions of service now require them to be available to discuss childrens' work with parents. Annual or termly parents' evenings remain one of the most frequent ways of meeting this requirement, but are not always satisfactory either for teachers or for parents. More frequent and more informal meetings generally provide more effective communication. These often take place in infant schools when parents collect their children from school. For older juniors a conscious decision to involve parents in project or topic work can be helpful, for example by enlisting their support in obtaining materials or information out of school. By helping to avoid an exclusive division between the child's life at home and at school, teachers can facilitate learning transfer, thus helping children to use their understanding, knowledge and skills in different contexts. In addition the benefits arising from parents' participation in the curriculum also apply in less structured contexts.

We have already noted the potential conflict between the values held by teachers and those held by parents. A further purpose of informal contacts between teachers and parents is to allow opportunities for sharing their respective expectations and hopes with respect to children's social development as well as their educational progress. By sharing these, they become more explicit. In turn, this enables teachers to establish links between the child's lives at home and at school. Interestingly, young children seen quite skilled at making these links. Edwards (1988) demonstrated the ability of 4 year-olds to distinguish between appropriate behaviour and feelings at home and at school.

In most cases a climate of trust and confidence can be achieved when parents visit the school. There are, however, occasions when parents cannot visit the school, either because they are working or because they are suffering from poor health. There are also occasions when teachers may feel that a child's welfare requires a closer understanding of the child's problems than is possible in the more formal setting of the school. In such circumstances a home visit can be useful. Home visiting is not something that all teachers find easy. Visiting with a more experienced colleague can be helpful on the first two or three occasions.

Marland (1985) lists four advantages in discussing a child's welfare in her or his own home. They are:

(i)   The school's representative has demonstrated sufficient concern to visit, and this fact alone is encouraging to parents or guardians;

(ii)   the pupil's parents or guardians are on *their* home ground, offering *their* hospitality, and this often gives them an added confidence and willingness to share;

(iii) in the home, the centrality of the pupil is symbolically more obvious and powerful than in school, where convenience of the school's system can loom larger;

(iv)   only in the pupil's own home setting is it possible to really learn about her or his background sympathetically, and to learn from parents or guardians (p. 106).

Conclusions

We have argued that schools have an inevitable impact on their pupils' personal and social development simply because pupils attend them. The impact may not be in the desired direction. In a devastating attack on much contemporary schooling Hargreaves (1982) claims that the secondary school system exerts on many pupils:

a destruction of their dignity which is so massive and so pervasive that few subsequently recover from it (p. 17).

The principal victims, he claims, are working-class children. Hargreaves may perhaps be unfair to secondary teachers but is certainly uncritical of primary education. Tizard and Hughes (1984) demonstrated that nursery school teachers consistently underestimated the ability of working-class children. They also showed, incidentally, that children's language experience was often richer at home than at school. Tizard *et al.* (1988) showed a similar tendency to underestimate working-class children's ability among infant teachers. The origins of the low self-esteem and chronic underachievement which Hargreaves indentifies in secondary schools are evident many years earlier.

Yet teachers unquestionably aim to raise children's self-esteem. They seek to do this by enhancing their feelings of personal involvement in classroom activities, as well as by giving them recognition as individual members of a class. Against these liberal aims stand the teacher's need for control and society's expectations with respect both to children's behaviour and to their educational progress. This is perhaps the major dilemma of contemporary schooling. The social interactionist view of learning that we have advocated in Chapters 4–6 may not solve this dilemma but we believe it goes some way towards doing so.

In other words, we should be cautiously optimistic. The principal theme of this chapter is that schools can contribute in constructive ways to their pupils' personal and social development. Yet the fact that they will inevitably have an effect shows why education is, and will remain a topic of interest to politicians as well as to psychologists. Bluntly, politicians may well be interested in the skills and knowledge that are taught through the National Curriculum but they will be much more interested, irrespective of party, in the values and attitudes that schools develop in their pupils. In other words their principal interest is in pupils' personal and social development.

In a democracy it is, of course, wholly inappropriate for teachers and school governors to follow blindly the biases and prejudices of the party in power. This would be a unreasonable as basing everything that happens in education on one particular school of psychological thought. Nevertheless, there is now a solid body of research to support the political pressure for teachers to establish closer and more effective partnerships with their pupils' parents. Equally, our knowledge of the way young children learn suggests that they adapt rapidly and apparently effortlessly to different situations. Personal and social education is bound up with notions of behaviour, attitudes and values. These cannot be compartmentalised. They develop from children's overall experience in the family, the school and elsewhere. For teachers this implies that personal and social education should be regarded as an integral part of the curriculum. To do so requires a policy for the whole school as well as for each class. The demands on teachers are considerable, but this is central to children's experience at school.

Notes and further reading

1. For further reading in personal and social education see:
   Hargreaves, A. *et al.* (1988) *Personal and Social Education: Choices and Challenges.* Oxford, Basil Blackwell.
   Pring, R.A. (1984) *Personal and Social Education in the Curriculum.* London, Hodder and Stoughton.
   Lang, P. (ed.) (1988) *Thinking about Personal and Social Education in the Primary School.* Oxford, Basil Blackwell.
   David, K. and Charlton, T. (eds.) (1987) *The Caring Role of the Primary School.* London, Macmillan.

2. The essential point here is that children, like adults, attribute causes to their experiences of success or failure. The nature of their attributions affects their subsequent motivation to attempt a task. See Weiner, B. (1979) A Theory of Motivation for Some Classroom Experiences. *Journal of Education Psychology*, 71, 3–25.

3. Weiner, B. (1984) Principles for a Theory of Student Motivation and their Application within an Attributionist Framework. In Ames, R.E. and Ames C. (eds.) *Research on Motivation in Education. Vol 1: Student Motivation.* London, Academic Press.

4. This perspective on the origins of universal compulsory education is described in greater detail by:
   Rubinstein, D. (1969) *School Attendance in London, 1870–1904: A Social History.* Hull, University of Hull.
   Humphries, S. (1981) *Hooligans or Rebels? An Oral History of Working Class Childhood and Youth, 1889–1939.* Oxford, Blackwell.

5. For reviews of research on the effectiveness of psychological treatments with different groups of children, see:
   Levitt, E.E. (1963) Results of Psychotherapy with Children: a further evaluation. *Behaviour, Research and Therapy*, 1, 45–51.
   Kolvin, I., Garside, R.D., Nicol, A.R., Macmillan, A., Wolstenholme, F. and Leitsch, I.M. (1981) *Help Starts Here: The Maladjusted Child in the Ordinary School.* London, Tavistock.

6. The hidden curriculum is too often regarded as an inevitably negative influence on children's development. For an alternative view see Roberts, I. (1979) The Hidden Curriculum in the Infants' School. *Durham and Newcastle Research Review*, 8, 42, 29–33.

Seminar suggestions

1. Make a detailed record of the activities of one child, or of a small group of children in the course of one section of the school day (e.g. arrival to the end of mid-morning play-time, or the end of mid-morning play-time to the end of dinner). As far as possible, record everything the children do *and* the instructions they receive from their teacher, the questions they are asked, etc. In the seminar examine these records and consider what the children may be learning through the hidden curriculum. What effects is this learning likely to have on their personal and social development?

2. Read the article by Tessa Roberts (1979). Now describe a child whom you regard as 'difficult' and discuss ways in which you could change this child's status in the class.

3. Plan a health education programme for one year group, integrating it with the projects/themes the class will be following during the year. Indicate how the content of this programme will 'mesh' with that of the previous year group and the following one.

Assessment and evaluation

The relationship between assessment and evaluation

Both the assessment of pupil performance and the evaluation of teacher action are central to the models of interactive pedagogy we have been discussing. The assessment of pupils' performance on task is essential to the planning of future learning experiences. While frequently referred to as informal classroom assessment, this process serves two useful purposes. It may be diagnostic, in the sense that it can reveal to the teacher/assessor strengths and weaknesses in a child's understanding or mastery of concepts or skills. It is formative, both in the sense that it focuses on the acquisition of skills and concepts and in the way that it is consequently used to inform teacher decision making in task setting. The assessment of pupils is therefore an integral element in the evaluation processes employed by teachers when reviewing their own pedagogical practices.

Assessment of pupils and evaluation of the curriculum can go hand in hand. When we look at the lesson plan outlined in Chapter 6, we can see that the decision to move pupils from the introduction of new skills or information alongside the teacher on to the opportunity to make sense of something on their own, is governed by teacher assessment of the extent to which the child appears to have grasped elements of the initial introduction. Similarly decisions on the need for extensive sense making experiences are informed by assessment of performance on tasks set by the teacher. Finally, judgements on mastery are made when children are engaged in more routine practice activities. At the same time as assessing performance on tasks, teachers evaluate the tasks themselves. They query whether the activities are actually providing children with the intended learning experiences and whether the appropriate amount of instruction has been given at the right time and pace. Continuous, formative assessment, supported by evaluations of pedagogy, therefore, underpin what is described as good primary practice.[1]

Assessment and evaluation in the 1990s

These two issues both dominate and are dominated by the implementation of a national curriculum in British primary schools.

The introduction of a nationally-applied set of curriculum guidelines which are sustained by a hierarchically-organised set of expected levels of pupil attainment have imposed a particular form of assessment on primary practice. An important and related evaluation issue also arises. The latter is best summarised by Holt (1987) when he criticises the 'mechanistic assumption that schools can be run like biscuit factories'. Holt objected to the simplistic view of evaluation which is encouraged by such a clearly defined national curriculum, as this is based on the belief that if schools are provided with equipment and targets, appropriate products will emerge. An alarming consequence of such a view of evaluation is that performance of pupils against nationally prescribed targets can provide the sole basis for judging schools. Here assessment and evaluation are closely linked, but not necessarily with the processes of pupil learning in mind.

Assessment

A Martian on a flying visit to Britain in the latter part of the 1980s may well have been excused the opinion that the introduction of a national curriculum was in fact the introduction of a national system of assessment. In 1985 'Better Schools' set the tone with:

The Government's central aim is to improve standards in schools, using the available resources to yield the best possible returns (DES, 1985, p. 90).

Clearly mindful of the view that the assessment system drives the task system, the assessment tail was set in motion to wag the curriculum dog.

An example of the rigidity deemed necessary to ensure curriculum uniformity was the organisation of levels of pupil attainment into specific linear hierarchies of progression. The simple linear model for attainment targets was not the only option available. Noss, Goldstein and Hoyles (1989) observed that it might have been preferable to have mapped out a range of possible routes for the learner. However, the prescribed pathway through the curriculum has been clearly way-marked by assessible criteria of performance at specific levels on each attainment target.

The result at a classroom level is that teachers are faced not only with a clearly defined body of knowledge and skills into which pupils should be inducted, but also a clearly delineated order of acquisition, which may not, in reality, match the order in which children do make sense of events (see Driver, (1983), on children's acquisition of scientific knowledge).

The importance of the way-marks, in the form of levels of attainment, may present the greatest obstacle to the success of the National Curriculum. Performance-based criteria ensure that a curriculum is reduced to a minimal set of learning objectives and that considerable teacher time is given to rigorous assessment at these significant points. Broadfoot (1988) looks to the experience of the United States in this area and notes the lack of relationship between improvements in test scores and an emphasis on testing. Indeed the United States experience suggests that time involved in testing and the high drop out rate of weaker students has resulted in a move towards an appreciation of teacher professionalism and away from control through testing. The control issue, implicit in a national testing programme, is important, particularly so when it relates to evaluation of learning experiences.[2]

Evaluation

The evaluation systems found in schools tend to serve a variety of purposes. Bates (1984) categorised these as pedagogical, individual development, organisational development and accountability. The pedagogical level provides the basis for the curricular decision making we have already described. The role of evaluation in the development of the individual teacher and the organisation has been a feature of much educational discussion in the 1970s and 1980s (e.g. Stenhouse, 1975, Skilbeck, 1984 and Simons, 1987). It now appears that the accountability aspects of evaluation may be increased by the introduction of a centrally orchestrated assessment system for primary schools.

The connection between assessment and evaluation is a complex one. Goldstein (1987 and 1988) points to the dangers of simplistic comparison of schools by results, given the general acceptance that the achievement of pupils on entry to a school is the most important predictor of later achievement. Consequently Goldstein claims that comparisons of schools should be based on the progress made by pupils. Whether the simple outcome measure or a more subtle gauge of progress is taken as the criterion, it seems likely that institutional evaluation will necessarily have some focus on those elements of pupil performance which are highlighted by the National Curriculum.

The purposes of assessment

The use of assessment for social control is not a phenomenon unique to the 1990s. As we have already mentioned in Chapter 5, the origins of Binet's intelligence testing lie in the need to 'normalise' the educational performance of pupils. Slightly later developments in the United States used intelligence testing as the basis for sorting children into streams or 'tracks' through schooling (Chapman, 1981), while after the Second World War intelligence testing in the UK became the acceptable device for the selection of pupils for specific forms of schooling.

Intelligence testing is the prime example of normative assessment in which the concern is to gauge the performance of a child against what might normally be expected of a child of a similar age. The notion of above or below average performance results as child is compared against child, usually for purposes of selection, guidance and prediction of future performance.

Standardised tests, most commonly used for assessing reading performance, are the norm-referenced tests most familiar to teachers. Rigour in administration is crucial and administration is often time-consuming. The results of the most frequently used reading tests, usually a reading age score which can be compared with the expected performance at the child's chronological age, assist in labelling the child as a good or poor reader but do nothing to either indicate causes of poor performance, e.g. whether they are primarily motivational or skills-based or to isolate areas of particular weakness (see Pumfrey, 1979 and Vincent *et al.*, 1983). Of more assistance to teachers in their planning of programmes for pupils is the use of diagnostic techniques, e.g. miscue analysis (Moyle, 1979; Moon, 1984), which provide the information on strengths and weaknesses crucial to the provision of further learning experiences.

Miscue analysis in fact belongs in the category of assessment techniques also occupied by the levels of attainment prescribed by the National Curriculum assessment programme. Criterion-referenced testing, where each child is assessed on the ability to master a particular skill or concept, is generally considered to be of more relevance to both the child's progress and teacher evaluation of the curriculum. Criterion-referenced assessment is therefore generally regarded to offer opportunities for diagnostic work and for isolating instructional needs as well as indicating to the teacher the progress of pupils and the efficacy of the curriculum.

The most commonly-found forms of criterion-referenced assessment have appeared in early years education. These include screening techniques (see Evans and Ferguson, 1974, for an overview of early attempts at this), nationally available checklists of which the Keele Pre-school Assessment Guide (Tyler, 1980) is a good example, and LEA or school-based behavioural checklists which reflect the institutional and curriculum priorities of specific groups of teachers or of an individual. As these checklists all relate to children's actions or performances in classrooms they have helped to hasten a move away from the physical, social and emotional priorities of post-war early years education to an emphasis on cognition and skills.

More recently, behavioural or criterion-based assessments have been developed in specific subject areas and have found their way into junior schools. Harlen's work has been influential in the area of primary science (Harlen *et al.*, 1977) and a useful overview of development in the criterion-referencing of primary science has been put together by the Association for Science Education (ASE, 1988). Several primary mathematics schemes have integral assessment programmes and the Inner London Education Authority is only one of many Local Education Authorities which have responded to the need for clearer criteria for the assessment of language skills. (ILEA, 1988).

As we have already mentioned, with reference to the National Curriculum, the relationship between curriculum, children's learning and criteria for assessment is not unproblematic, and care needs to be taken to ensure that teachers are alert to the fact that children's progress through curriculum areas may not always match the set linear pattern suggested by neat lists of criteria. As Harlen (1989), points out, a child's performance on a process skill, e.g. planning an investigation, will depend to some extent on the child's familiarity with the material under investigation.

While outlining the distinctions between the purposes of norm-referenced and criterion-referenced assessments we have also begun to focus on the difference between two other purposes of assessment in schools. That is whether it is summative or formative. If assessment is essentially for the purposes of selection, long-term prediction or reporting and asks the question 'how well has the child done?' either in comparison with other children, or at the end of a programme of study, the assessment is generally regarded as summative and usually enters the public domain to become available, often for reporting purposes, to parents, other colleagues, the LEA, and so on. If on the other hand, assessment is used to inform pedagogy and asks the question 'how is the child making sense of this?' it is generally considered to be formative in nature, providing vital feedback on pupil strengths and weaknesses, and is usually initially private, remaining the direct concern of the teacher, who responds to this information with appropriate experiences for the child.

Formative assessment is not necessarily diagnostic, as diagnostic assessment may require the teacher to delve more deeply into a child's misconceptions (see Bennett *et al.*, 1984), but diagnostic assessment is certainly formative. The Task Group in Assessment and Testing (TGAT) suggest that the boundary between formative and diagnostic purposes is not sharp or clear (DES, 1988d, para. 27) but that while diagnostic assessment may sometimes be necessary, it leads to more information that may usefully be passed on to another teacher (DES, 1988d, para. 27). Nevertheless formative and diagnostic assessment do gather vital information on the progress of children through a curriculum programme and therefore eventually need to be collated into a form which will be relatively quick to read and eventually make sense to other colleagues, particularly to the teacher of the next year group, and so facilitate continuity in the child's learning from year to year.

Formative assessment then, provides useful information at summative stages. Clearly, however, summative assessment is not produced through the simple accumulation of formative assessments. The concern of summative assessment is mainly to report what the child is capable of doing at a certain point in his or her school life.

Record keeping

Record keeping systems therefore need to provide a bridge between curricular demands and children's learning in ways which both immediately assist teachers' task setting and are amenable to summary for reporting purposes. If we take to heart the belief that the assessment system leads the task system, it is crucial that the record of assessment is itself driven by the pedagogy which underpins classroom practice.

If the lesson plan outlined in Chapter 6 is adopted, a record keeping system needs to reflect the teacher's concern with the stages leading to mastery, i.e. initial experience, making sense and practice. The National Curriculum has removed curriculum content from the area of debate, as assessment now focuses on levels and statements of attainment on specified curricular targets. A record keeping system based on these principles may look like Table 8.1.

Table 8.1 **A sample record keeping system**

Science	Child A	Child B	Child C
AT 1			
Level 1	⊘	⊘	⊘
Level 2	⊘	⊘	
Level 3	✓		
AT 2			

Key ✓ = has had initial experience
O = making sense – more opportunity for use needed in different contexts
\ = has mastered

This is a far cry from a simple record of the child's experience in particular curriculum areas and raises issues of both mastery and context in the assessment of pupils in classrooms.

Assessing pupils

As Harlen (1989) has already indicated, mastery of skills is not a simple issue, but may be affected by a child's familiarity with the material to which the skill is to be applied.

In addition, most teachers are only too aware of the loss of learning that can occur, even over a half-term break. Consequently it is important to err on the side of caution when assuming mastery and to ensure that skills and understanding can be demonstrated in a variety of contexts wherever possible.

The Primary Language Record developed by the Inner London Education Authority's Centre for Language in Primary Education (ILEA, 1988) operates a diary structure and provides a checklist matrix which reminds teachers to note the social context (e.g. pair, small group, or with adult) and the learning context (e.g. play, drama, story telling, Maths and Science investigation or design, construction craft and art projects) in which the observed behaviour occurs. The accompanying diary record serves as a basis for the planning of future experiences and can be summarised into a profile of the 'child as language user' for reporting and discussion with parents.

The contexts within which assessments are made are clearly important. Donaldson (1978) alerted teachers to children's abilities to pick up perceptual cues which may distort their readings of task demands, while motivational factors relating to confidence may also be at work. Edwards (1984, 1988) observed that children as young as four years of age had clear ideas about their own competencies in specific areas of the nursery school.

One way of addressing both the mastery and context issues is to gather information on pupil performance from as wide a range of sources as possible. Teachers have been doing this for years through the examination of children's written work, observation of performance on task, listening to children's questions and eavesdropping on children's conversations while they are on task. With national guidelines on learning objectives, the focus of the observations is clearly and uniformly prescribed, consequently the teacher's gaze or ear is geared to note specific aspects of performance. But is it as simple as that? There are several important issues to consider when assessing children's performance on task.

A first concern must be whether we are actually witnessing the child's optimal performance. Has the child in Doyle's terms bid the task down to a low risk activity? (see Chapters 4 and 5). There is many a working parent who can make a good lasagne, but who will microwave a supermarket version at the end of a heavy day. On which 'performance' as chef should she/he be judged? A second issue is whether the child has actually picked out the salient aspect of the task. How easily can a task which is intended by a teacher to provide opportunity for exercising abilities in the area of measuring and understanding of shape be seen as a colouring task by a child?

While these two problems can be overcome through careful goal setting and resourcing, the fundamental issue is the relationship between task setting and assessment. Here we meet an aspect of curriculum planning which is perhaps more open to debate in primary schools than in secondary schools.

Topic work, whether central or peripheral to curriculum planning is, at the very least, an accepted way of operating a curriculum in primary schools. Indeed assessment guidelines, (e.g. DES, 1989c) are premised on the belief that topic work features large in the education of the under 12s. The key assessment issue in topic based work is the extent to which the task system is directed by assessment demands. In practical terms this is a question of whether topics are designed with statements of attainment clearly in mind or whether topics evolve from more spontaneous interests and opportunities requiring teachers to be ever mindful of attainment targets and levels while observing children.

These two routes to achieving evidence of attainment represent differing views of the curriculum, but make some similar demands on teachers. Both require a good grasp of possible performance criteria, a record keeping system which is appropriate and a means of bringing some rigour to the information collection process.

Such rigour may simply require a sharpening of the looking and listening expertise of teachers already outlined. As we noted in Chapter 5 primary teachers are by tradition and training good observers of children. Sadly the National Curriculum requirements demand a narrowing of focus to concentrate the gaze on specific competencies. A consequent danger may be a fragmented view of the child in which attention to socio-emotional and physical aspects of the child's development becomes separated from attention to academic achievement. Record keeping systems necessarily help in the selection of the assessment focus, consequently a recognition of the need to create a well-balanced profile of each child may counteract the possible narrowing of interest.

The assessment skills already available to primary school teachers are shown in Table 8.2.

The techniques we have suggested demonstrate the wide variety of ways in which teachers can use existing skills and collect evidence of children's competencies in a relatively rigorous manner. Photographs of prototypes and completed constructions and examples of children's written planning or final products not only serve as more lasting reminders of children's competencies but may be selectively retained to supplement profiles of children's progress through the curriculum.

Tape recordings may be used for similar purposes but are more likely to be of use when providing evidence of children's abilities without the presence of the teacher. Open-ended but carefully

Table 8.2 *Using teacher skills in assessing children's work*

Teacher skills	Applications	Techniques	Weaknesses
Observation skills	Activities involving selection of resources, construction, sorting, some planning activities.	Diary notes, checklists, photographs.	Teacher can miss points when 'distracted' 'Doing' doesn't necessarily mean full understanding.
Listening skills	Activities involving oracy skills demonstrating understanding of concepts, e.g. through giving explanations or planning.	Diary notes, checklists, tape recordings, diagnostic 'conversations'.	Difficult to get close to children without interrupting. Teacher questions can lead responses. Children can be wary of teacher questions and under-perform.
Marking written skills	Activities involving writing and including cloze procedures, plans and simple paper and pencil tests.	Diary notes, checklists, examples of children's work.	Children's written explanations do not do justice to their conceptual understanding. Can force an emphasis on the final product to the detriment of the quality of the process skills.

resourced problem-solving tasks may seem suited to this method of information collection. However, the danger here is that there may be the need for a lot of teacher listening time in order to catch a few pieces of hard evidence. Indeed it appears that this method works best when a simple task, e.g. weighing or sorting, is set, or when children are asked to engage in a specific planning activity perhaps relating to oracy skills and story telling. Another good use of the tape recorder is, to supply a child or pair of children with a task and an instruction card which requires them to record responses at certain key points during the task.

What is evident from Table 8.2 is that no assessment skill or technique is without its problems. Therefore, we return to the point made earlier, that it is necessary to collect information in a variety of ways and in different contexts.

Profiles and records of achievement

It is interesting to observe the development of pupil profiling in secondary schooling during the 1980s. Profiles emerged as a heartfelt response to what is frequently described as the pernicious effects of the secondary school examination system . which was regarded as depersonalising and demotivating. A range of models for profiles were created (see Law, 1984, for an overview). While all shared a common emphasis on building a rounded and developmental picture of the pupil they differed in the amount of responsibility for assessment given to pupils, parents and teachers. In some cases they were jointly controlled by pupil and teacher and assessments negotiated between both. Other models represented an extension of the more traditional teacher reporting and others supplemented this method with supplied teacher comments from comment banks in attempts to avoid what was regarded by some as the subjectivity of negotiated assessment or the idiosyncracies of teachers' own written comments.

The control of profiles in an interesting area which can only be briefly addressed here. (See Hargreaves, 1986, for a critical perspective on the profiling movement.) Nevertheless, it is important to consider the pedagogical implications of jointly negotiated assessments particularly when this is considered in the light of the emphasis we have given to classroom interactions and negotiations around task setting in earlier chapters of this book. Indeed, jointly controlled assessments under a profiling scheme may have considerable effect on the teaching-learning interaction in classrooms as goals and interpretations are more fully explained.

Once again we have an example of how the assessment system may be used to lead the task system, as this particular form of assessment may induct children into metacognitive reflection on their own learning processes. The use of profiles and records of achievement fits well with the framework for assessment underpinning this chapter. We have differentiated between formative and summative assessment, and have more finely explored the difference between diagnostic and more general formative statements of pupil achievements. We have been suggesting that detailed record keeping based on formative assessment is necessary for effective lesson planning and task setting but that these are essentially private documents of use primarily to the class teacher. They do, however, provide the information which may be distilled into more general developmental profiles which allow an accumulative record of the child's progress through schooling as she or he moves from term to term and from class to class.

Profiles in primary schools, therefore, usually hold summative information for more public consumption by parents and by colleagues within and outside the primary school. While currently formats vary there is generally an emphasis on producing a well-balanced view of the primary school child which allows consideration not only of academic progress but also of social and physical development. As the portrait is cumulative extending throughout the child's school life, another concern is simplicity and readability and the appropriateness of the design for both school entry and transfer requirements. These summaries of progress are often supplemented by the hard evidence, for example of selections of pupil products or photographs of work in progress. In this way information used for more detailed formative assessment is used to illuminate and give depth to the profile portraits.[3]

Clearly profiles serve an important purpose but need to be seen as simply a method of reporting pupil progress. Assessment occurs during the daily processes of classroom life and needs to be recorded in ways which support the daily professional decision making of teachers.

Self-evaluation in classrooms

Earlier in this chapter we touched upon the problems of accountability inherent in too simplistic a view of the relationship between pupil performance and the evaluation of curricular institutions or the practice of teaching. The relationship between assessment and evaluation is in fact a subtle one and may be seen as empowering for both pupil and teacher.

Evaluation is essentially a simple process, best illustrated as a cycle of plan, act and review:

Figure 8.1 *The plan, act, review cycle*

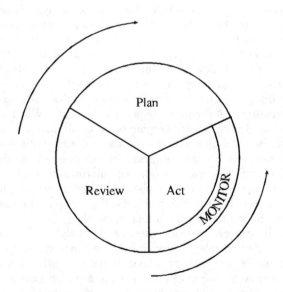

Planning involves setting clear, achievable goals. This is followed by taking action which is aimed at ensuring the realisation of these goals, monitoring that action and finally reviewing the outcome of the action in terms of the original goals. The review stage demands reflection on whether or not the goals set have been met and the reasons for whatever disparity exists. This reflection forms the starting point for planning the next action stage.

This model of evaluation is frequently used by teachers in the daily monitoring and planning of classroom tasks. Interestingly it also can provide a useful framework for pupils' management of their own learning. As we outlined in Chapter 1, major themes in this volume include pupil motivation, metacognition, or reflection on one's own learning, and self-evaluation. We can begin to see how they are closely related. To return to a point we have already made several times, clearly defined goals have to be linked to an interactive model of pedagogy if children are to perform to the best of their ability in any curricular area. When this is considered using the language of evaluation we are suggesting that goals are clearly set or negotiated and that pupil progression towards goals may be monitored by both teachers and the pupils themselves. Also the degree of success as the goal is reached is open to evaluation by pupils. Self-evaluating pupils therefore are able to take greater responsibility for their own learning processes (see Nisbet and Shucksmith, 1986). Similarly, as we have already argued, self-evaluating teachers are more likely to feel in control of their own decision making. Taylor (1977) points to a strong and important link between responsibility, self-evaluation and action and motivation, regarding the opportunity to take responsibility for evaluations of one's own actions as crucial to motivation. Edwards (1988) related this to schools in terms of the quality of the relationship between learner and teacher. Motivating children by allowing them increasing responsibility for their own evaluations requires a delicate handling of interactions and the avoidance of overtly judgemental behaviours on the part of the teacher.

It may be unfair to ask practitioners to assess without being judgemental. Nevertheless, the demotivating effect of depressed pupil self-esteem due to experience of failure needs to be considered. Careful match of task and child based on assessment of learning needs should help avoid situations in which self-esteem is threatened by failure on task, while clear goal setting encourages pupil self-evaluation. Some of the difficulties of an over-emphasis on assessment nevertheless do continue as teachers are under pressure to produce good pupil performances in specific areas of the curriculum to satisfy the external evaluations of their pedagogy and of their institutions.

For both pupils and teachers the route to a feeling of effectiveness is a feeling of control over processes and outcomes or put more simply, the ability to predict future results. We all know the apprehension with which we approach for example a new and complex appliance or tackle a new recipe which demands untested skills. We fear the possibility of our own ineffectiveness, and may delay tackling the new appliance or decide to try out the recipe for our nearest and dearest before risking the demonstration of our ineptitude to the wider world. We have already noted in Chapter 5 that a pupil response to this kind of challenge in classrooms is to attempt to remove the risk, by bidding down the task, so that instead of being a challenge it becomes routine. If, as teachers, we want to keep some element of challenge in some tasks, we need to provide pupils with coping strategies which allow them to keep the activity within their control. One way is to allow them to take responsibility for some evaluations. As we have already suggested, the learning strategies outlined by Nisbet and Shucksmith (1986) and summarised in the notion of 'planfulness', fit well with the plan, act, review cycle and allow the child to break activities into manageable stages of e.g. planning, monitoring, checking, revising and self-testing (Nisbet and Shucksmith, 1986, p. 28).

Similarly teachers may feel overwhelmed or pressured by the challenging demands of a nationally imposed and planned curriculum. One way of keeping a grip on process in a time of change has always been to self-monitor, to use consistently the plan, act, review cycle when initiating change in the classroom. With the increase in accountability through the implementation of a national curriculum and to an extent through teacher appraisal there is also a need to be increasingly articulate in the justification of pedagogic practices. Regular use of the evaluation cycle with its emphasis on monitoring and reflection on action, allows practitioners to stand back and examine their own practices, to discover ways of explaining them and to keep a record of curricular and pedagogic decisions they have made. All three aspects empower teachers when they enter the arena of external or public evaluation of their teaching or institution.[4]

Teacher professionalism and accountability

The tension between public accountability and professional integrity can be seen in the areas of both assessment and evaluation. Both issues demand demonstration and public recognition of teachers' professional competence. Without public recognition of their professional competence in the areas of assessment and evaluation, teachers will be unable to resist further intervention by the government, or by the governors of their own school. Hard evidence will be needed. In the case of pupil assessment this will be found in the quality of the assessment process demonstrated in effective record keeping. In the case of evaluation, written records are also important. They need to be as simple and relevant, and take up as little time as possible. Models of teacher appraisal which are primarily concerned with staff development have already picked up on these points. Those appraisal systems which require the teacher to engage in self-evaluation prior to and during appraisal are premised on the belief that teachers need to enter into appraisal or external evaluation as active participants who see themselves – and are seen – as able to use the experience to extend their own understanding, and hence to increase the effectiveness of their teaching. Written evidence, such as a summary of a diary record of the monitoring of action, taken together with reflections and planning, provide an agenda for discussion. Consequently the professional is able to take some control over that agenda and discuss what she or he sees to be most relevant. Here we return to the notion of responsibility we have just discussed in connection with pupil learning. Logically this leads us to stress the importance of teachers also being responsible for their own evaluations of their actions if they are to take and pursue pedagogic decisions.

Further reading

1. An excellent introduction to assessment in primary schools is provided by: Shipman, M. (1983) *Assessment in Primary and Middle Schools*. London, Croom Helm.
    At a very practical level Duncan and Dunn's collection of ideas may prove helpful. (Duncan, A. and Dunn, W. (1988) *What Primary Teachers Should Know About Assessment*. London, Hodder and Stoughton.)
2. Several papers in a British Educational Research Association publication elaborate the debates surrounding assessment in primary schools: Torrance, H. (ed.) (1988) *National Assessment and Testing: A Research Response* British Educational Research Association. But the context of much of the discussion on assessment has been secondary schools. Points made in these analyses are relevant to aspects of assessment in primary schools and are therefore worth pursuing, for example:
    Black, H.D. and Dockrell, W.B. (eds.) (1988) *New Developments in Educational Assessment*. Edinburgh, Scottish Academic Press.
    Brown, M. (1989) Graded Assessment and Learning Hierarchies in Mathematics – an Alternative View. *British Educational Research Journal*, 15, 2, 121–8.
    These both examine some of the current technical topics in the area of testing.
    Broadfoot, again with largely a secondary school focus, explores historical, cross-cultural and the more general sociological issues relating to assessment. (Broadfoot, P. (ed.) (1984) *Selection, Certification and Control: Social Issues in Educational Assessment*. Lewes, Falmer Press.
3. A useful practical guide to developing records of achievement is found in: Pritchard, K. and Richmond, K. (1989) *The Records of Achievement Manual*. York, Longman. Again the context is secondary education, but

the processes outlined and ideas provided may be easily transferred.

Broadfoot gives a wide ranging overview of developments in records of achievement at both a practical and critical level (Broadfoot, P. (ed.) (1986) *Profiles and Records of Achievement: A Review of Issues and Practice*. Eastbourne, Holt, Rinehart and Winston.)

4.   A good introduction to issues relating to school, curriculum and teacher evaluation is provided by: Horton, T. and Raggatt, P. (eds.) (1982) *Challenge and Change in the Curriculum*. London, Hodder and Stoughton.

Similarly important basic issues, relating institutional and self-evaluation to accountability are raised in: Nuttall, D. (1981) *School Self-Evaluation: Accountability with a Human Face*. London, Schools Council.

For a primary school based introduction to teacher self-evaluation see: Pollard, A. and Tann, S. (1987) *Reflective Teaching in the Primary School*. London, Cassell.

Suggestions for seminar activities

1.   Ask students to think of an activity they have recently planned, given, or might consider giving to a group of children in a primary classroom. It can be mundane or imaginative, for example writing news, measuring the playground, making a skeleton. Ask them to list the competencies (skills/understanding) that the children may demonstrate on that task. Then ask students to focus on one or two competences and decide on how they would assess mastery of the competency, for example through observation, examination of written work?

   Discussion could focus on the need to isolate aspects of the child's performance when assessing, sharing these goals with the child, appropriate methods of assessing, building assessment into task planning, or avoiding waste of teacher time.

2.   Ask students to provide examples of children's work. (Equally these can be supplied by the tutor.) In each case the intended outcomes, or pedagogical purposes of the task should be made clear in an explanatory paragraph. Ask students to work in pairs or threes to assess the child's performance on the task, answering the question 'what is it evident that the child can do?'. Then ask each pair or triad to note the difficulties they have had with the task. In a final plenary discussion the following issues could be raised: the importance of relationships to our assessment of children, for example, how well we know the child, expectations we hold, the assessment skills teachers possess and use without self-awareness, the need to be clear about intended task outcomes, agreement on mastery of a competency, the 'whole child' view of primary education, the irrelevance of the age of the child to criterion referenced testing, implications for record keeping.

3.   Ask students to think of an activity they have planned recently for a group of children. Ask them to identify the aim of the activity, and of how they knew that the aim had been met (or not), what they as teachers had learnt from setting that task and how they might do it differently next time. Discuss the importance of monitoring and collecting evidence about the action taken to provide a focus for reflection and planning and remind

students of ways in which evidence may be collected, for example, observations, diary, tape recording, photographs, children's work, talking with children or parents. Provide groups of three students with large sheets of paper and pens and ask them to work through the plan, act, review cycle on one of the activities described, this time emphasising how and where evidence may be collected, for example what needs to be considered at the planning stage, where can evidence be gathered? What is an appropriate way of monitoring the activity, and one which does not take up too much teacher time? Who can help with the review or reflection stage? What do you really need to know at that stage? Were the aims clearly stated at the planning stage? The session could finish with a discussion on either the importance of having clear aims in order to evaluate effectively, or on appropriate methods of monitoring actions.

CHAPTER 9

Conclusions

Theory and classroom practice: An interactive relationship

Chapter 1 argued that theories provide starting points from which we can begin to reflect on, monitor and evaluate our own experience. This is particularly true when their theoretical underpinning enables researchers to obtain results the significance of which extends beyond the research sample itself. Examples are Bennett's work on matching the difficulty of the task to the ability of the pupil (Bennett et al., 1984, Chapter 5), the extensive investigations into time on task (Chapter 6) and the even more extensive investigations into applied behaviour analysis (Chapter 6).

Yet the relationship is not one-way. The problems teachers face in the classroom can also provoke theoretical advances. The Warnock Report's conclusion that up to 20 per cent of children could be said to have special educational needs (DES, 1978a) and the claim of HMI in Scotland that up to 50 per cent of pupils could be said to have learning difficulties (Scottish Education Department 1978) directed both professional and political attention to the needs of academically less able pupils. Nevertheless, it was the experience of teachers in mainstream schools that provided the impetus for a radical reformulation of the scope and aims of education for the children concerned, with consequent developments in the conceptual framework for its provision.

In other words theory and research interact with classroom practice. This view can be looked at in two ways. First, although politicians play a part – often an unhealthily large part – in determining the allocation of research funds, in practice research teams have to modify their agenda in the light of teachers' current interests. The reason is simply that teachers quite reasonably withhold active cooperation from researchers who are not addressing their legitimate concerns. Secondly, and more importantly, the models of teaching and learning that we have proposed in this book place the teacher in the role of researcher. The monitoring, re-appraisal and self-evaluation inherent in all effective teaching is essentially a research activity.[1]

Teachers as learners

The interactive relationship between teaching and researchers implies, then, that teachers influence the agenda for research, often after it has formally been defined by politicians or by researchers themselves. It also implies that teachers determine the nature of theoretical advances in the obvious, but important, sense that most major advances in school and teacher effectiveness have been based on researchers' observations of teachers at work. We have given particular emphasis to four themes throughout this book.

1. The influences on children's development are varied, and interact on each other. Returning to children with special needs, Rutter (1981) points out that children can cope with single, isolated sources of stress, however severe, if they really are isolated. In contrast, when sources of stress come in combination, for example when parental separation is combined with financial problems in the home, a change of house, death of a loved grandparent *and* a string of supply teachers in a school that suffers from weak leadership, the effects of each is likely to interact with and aggravate the other. Most teachers can think of children whose behaviour and progress have deteriorated when several things in their lives have gone wrong at the same time. Similarly, most can recognise the potential impact of culturally based expectations connected with gender, ethnicity and social class. Gender and ethnicity are currently politically more sensitive – or at least talked about more. On the other hand, it remains quite clear that children from working-class homes are likely to leave school with fewer qualifications than those from middle-class homes, irrespective of intellectual ability (e.g. Davie, Butler and Goldstein, 1972; Fogelman, 1976).

2. Teaching is an active process in which children and teachers interact with, and on, each other. Again, most teachers will recognise the reciprocity described, for example by Doyle (1986). The interaction can be constructive – a necessary and desirable aspect of working together on a shared task – or it can be restricting, as when children successfully negotiate down the difficulty of a task.

3. A hallmark of successful teaching is that children develop the metacognitive skills of reflecting critically on the nature of a task, monitoring the demands it makes and identifying appropriate ways to overcome them. However, children are only likely to acquire these skills when their teacher has acquired them, and uses them in her/his own teaching.

4. It follows from this that evaluation is central to all teaching activities. The evaluation can be carried out at several levels. Failure to differentiate adequately between the needs of different children or groups of children can lead to unstimulating, undemanding tasks for able children and tasks which less able children find too difficult. In other words attention focuses both on the abilities of the children and

on the difficulty of the task. At a slightly more complex level, failure to recognise our own personal biases, perhaps arising from cultural expectations linked to gender, race or social class, can lead us to expect too little of some children and, possibly, too much of others.

All this raises important questions about the applications of research. Clearly, there is no direct relationship between research findings and charges in professional practice. If all schools could become more effective simply by copying the most effective school described by Mortimore *et al.* (1988), teaching would be a boringly mechanistic and straightforward process. It manifestly is not! Hence we need to consider the processes that restrict and enhance our ability and/or willingness to learn from our own or other people's experience. The concept of motivational style is helpful here.

Motivation to learn: An attributionist perspective

Motivational style develops from teachers' and children's perceptions of the environment in which they work. According to Ames (1987) it is the systematic, qualitative response which individuals make to situations in which they judge success or failure to be possible. These perceptions are held to determine the 'style' of the individual' motivation. The concept of style is useful because it moves away from quantitative definitions of motivation such as time on task. Instead it sees children as actively involved in making choices about how they will behave. Galloway and Rogers (1990) have noted two forms of motivational style which have particular relevance for teachers.

'Learned helplessness'

Some children believe they are not clever enough to succeed on a task and rapidly give up. Because they attribute failure to lack of ability, their expectation of success rapidly declines: they do not believe there is any point in trying (see Dweck and Wortman, 1982). Dweck also identifies another group of children whom she defines as 'master oriented'. These children do not attribute failure to lack of ability: rather, when they have found something difficult they seek clues as to how they may improve their performance in future.

Self-worth motivation

Other children believe they *are* clever enough to succeed on a task but do not want to risk failure. Because being clever, successful or popular is important to their self-esteem they avoid situations in which their image of themselves could be threatened. For these children, the harder they try at a task, for example their part in the class project, the greater the threat to their self-esteem if they do not succeed. Primary teachers see this most vividly, and most frequently, in children with reading difficulties. A strategy which these children sometimes adopt is to protect themselves from failure by refusing to make any real effort, rationalising this on the grounds that they are not interested, or that they do not care.

A feature of motivational style of particular interest to primary teachers is that it probably becomes more pervasive *after* pupils transfer to secondary schools. In other words, children who show evidence of learned helplessness in one curriculum area or with one teacher may behave quite differently in other curriculum areas or with other teachers. Nicholls (1984) has suggested that motivational style crystallises around the age of 11. This could be due both to developmental factors and to changes in school organisation. Young children's conceptions of ability allows for the possibility that it may increase. After puberty they increasingly see ability as relatively fixed and stable. For primary teachers the encouraging implication is that they are likely to have a substantial influence on their pupils' motivational style.

As so often, children's strategies, or in this case motivational styles, have a parallel in those of their teachers. Learned helplessness is reflected in comments like 'he's just not very bright, and that's all there is to it', or 'her problem is her parents and we can't change *them*'. Such comments conceal a feeling that nothing the individual does will make any difference, either in the sense of eliciting support from senior colleagues or in terms of pupil progress. Ultimately this leads to loss of interest in the professional nature of the job and the feeling of apathy associated with 'burn-out'.[2]

Self-worth motivation, or more descriptively self-worth protection, is reflected in comments like: 'I *could* do something for Jenny but it wouldn't be fair on the others to give her so much time', or 'I *could* do something for Peter but it would be undermined by parental indifference, so there's no point'. Self-worth motivation is seen in teachers who hide behind their professional status to justify reluctance to evaluate their work. It may also be seen in teachers who use their perhaps legitimate sense of grievance about inadequate resources or poor conditions of service to justify low levels of involvement in their work.

Changing and/or maintaining motivational style

So far we have only drawn attention to the potentially restricting, negative effects of motivational style. Most teachers, though, approach their work in ways that create opportunities not only for their pupils but also for their own professional development, rather than restricting them in the way envisaged by learned helplessness and self-worth motivation. Hence, we need to ask how a positive motivational style can be maintained as well as how a less positive one may be changed.

Diener and Dweck (1978) demonstrated the possibility of reducing the effects of learned helplessness, at least in primary age boys. They gave children who had been identified as learned helpless a test on which failure was likely. They then told one group that they had not tried hard enough, and should make greater effort in a second test. The second group was told that the first test had been difficult, but was congratulated for trying. The theory of learned helplessness predicts that the second group's performance will deteriorate still further on the second test; because the teacher has reinforced their own belief in their lack of ability to influence what happens to them: if the task is likely to be difficult, there is no point in trying. In contrast the theory would predict that the first group might improve on the second test: the children had been told that their failure was something they *could* do something about, by trying harder. This, in fact, is what happened. The implication is that children who feel that *they* have some control over their own learning are likely to develop a sense of responsibility for it. In Doyle's (Doyle and Carter, 1984 and Doyle, 1986) terms children are more likely to take risks if they see their teacher as someone who helps them to achieve mastery in spite of the difficulties. In Nisbet and Shucksmith's (1986) terms, metacognitive skills give children a feeling of involvement in and responsibility for their work which is incompatible with the restrictions on development implicit in learned helplessness and self-worth motivation as described above.

There is a lack of systematic research on the motivational styles of teachers, let alone on ways of changing them. On the other hand, both anecdote and observation suggests that motivational style is not constant. Rather it responds to the quality of leadership and support from colleagues, and to the nebulous concept of school climate.

There is now a growing body of research on differences between schools in pupils' behaviour and educational progress, irrespective of the social background of the school's pupils. It is equally clear that schools are not static institutions. For better or worse, many schools vary over time in their effectiveness in achieving their educational and social goals. It is reasonable to suppose that developments in pupil performance reflect developments in teachers' motivation. One implication that merits further investigation is that motivational style may be related to the concepts of morale and job satisfaction.

A study of New Zealand primary teachers revealed significantly higher levels of job satisfaction among teachers whose principal (i.e. head teacher) was aged less than 50 than among teachers whose principal was aged 50 or more (Galloway *et al.*, 1985). David Galloway was unable to answer a barbed question at one conference, namely what proportion of each group of principal had served in the army before taking up teaching. The clear implication behind the question, though, was that the differences in teachers' job satisfaction could be related to the principal's management style.

This survey also provided an interesting insight on primary school principals. Those principals who were currently undertaking some form of advanced professional study, either through a university course or correspondence course, reported significantly higher job satisfaction than those who were not (Galloway *et al.*, 1986). The numbers were small, so conclusions must be tentative. We are not suggesting that if only all teachers would enrol for post-experience degree or diploma courses at their local college or university, the nation's educational problems would be solved. The possible implications are nevertheless interesting: (a) that advanced professional study may promote the model of the self-evaluating, questioning teacher that is implicit in so much of the work we have discussed in earlier chapters: (b) that this approach to teaching from senior staff promotes a positive motivational style, not only in the senior teachers themselves, but also in their colleagues and in pupils.

Overview

The usefulness of the work of academics studying the psychology of education may be judged largely by the extent to which it helps teachers to raise the quality of their work with children. The same is true of the work of educational psychologists employed by LEAs. Children's learning processes and the factors which influence them, are likely to retain a central place in the work of psychologists, as of teachers. In other words, teachers and psychologists have a shared interest in the influence on children's educational, personal and social development of schools as social organisations and of the classroom as an environment for learning.

The partnership between teaching and psychology has been a profitable one in the past. In the 1990s it will assume even greater importance. The 1980s saw central control of education increase beyond recognition, culminating in the 1988 Education Reform Act. The National Curriculum, local management of schools, the possibility of seeking grant-maintained status, increased parental freedom to select their child's school: these and other legislative changes were ostensibly motivated by a desire to raise educational standards. Yet legislation can do nothing more than provide the framework within which the education system develops. Development is not necessarily healthy, and as we have already noted it is too early to evaluate the impact of the 1988 Act.

Nevertheless, we feel no embarrassment in concluding with two observations. First, every LEA has plenty of examples of what HMI is pleased to call 'good practice', both at school and at classroom level. While the concept of good practice is contentious, not least because it varies over time,[3] the evidence that schools vary in their success in achieving common educational and social goals is now widely accepted. The evidence also suggests that variations between teachers within a school are at least as important as variation between schools. An increasingly clear picture is emerging of effective schools and of effective teachers. Secondly, the successful introduction of the National Curriculum, together with all the other changes the government imposed in the 1980s will demand an increasingly sophisticated understanding of teaching and learning processes. Substantial progress has been made. A disquieting characteristic of this progress is that the more we understand about teaching and learning the more clearly we recognise how much remains to be understood. This *is* disquieting, but it is also why most teachers enjoy their work: opportunities for personal and professional development continue throughout the individual's career. We hope this book will help to open up some of these opportunities.

Notes and suggestions for further reading

1. The notion of teachers as researchers is well developed in Stenshouse, L. (1975) *An Introduction to Curriculum Research and Development.* London, Heinemann.
2. The concept of burn-out is more fully explored in: Edelwick, J. and Brodsky, A. (1980) *Burn-out: Stages of Disullusionment in the Helping Professions.* New York, Human Sciences Press.
3. The controversies on what constitutes good practice are well analysed by: Knight, P. and Smith, L. (1989) In Search of Good Practice. *Journal of Curriculum Studies*, 21, 427–40.

Seminar suggestions

1. Debate the motion that: 'Public money spent on educational psychologists and on research into the psychology of education would be better spent in other ways'.
2. Think of two children you have taught whose behaviour is consistent with 'learned helplessness' or 'self-worth motivation' as described in the text. Be prepared to describe the children in the seminar, and discuss ways in which you might increase their motivation to attempt challenging tasks in the classroom.

REFERENCES

Ainscow, M. and Florek, A. (eds) (1989) *Special Educational Needs: Towards a Whole-School Approach*. London, David Fulton.

Ames, C. (1987) The Enhancement of Student Motivation. In M. Maehr and D.A. Kleiber (eds) *Enhancing Motivation*. Greenwich, Conn., JAI Press.

Anderson, E. (1973) *The Disabled Schoolchild; A Study of Integration in Primary Schools*. London, Methuen.

Anderson, L.W. (ed.) (1986) *Time and School Learning*. London, Croom Helm.

Apple, M. (1979) *Ideology and the Curriculum*. London, Routledge and Kegan Paul.

Apple, M. (1983) *Power and Education*. London, Routledge and Kegan Paul.

Apple, M. (1985) *Education and Power*. London, Ark.

Association for Science Education (ASE) (1988) *Initiatives in Primary Science: An Evaluation. Building Bridges*. Hatfield, ASE.

ASE (Association for Science Education together with Association of Teachers of Mathematics, Mathematical Association, and National Association for the teaching of English) (1989) *The National Curriculum – Making it work for the primary school*. Hatfield, ASE.

Ausubel, D. (1968) *Educational Psychology: A Cognitive View*. New York, Holt, Rinehart and Winston.

Bandura, A. (1974) Behaviour Theory and Models of Man. *American Psychologist*, 29, 859–69.

Bannister, D. and Fransella, F. (1971) *Inquiring Man: The Theory of Personal Constructs*. Harmondsworth, Penguin.

Barton, L. (1989) *Special Educational Needs: Myth or Reality?* Lewes, Falmer Press.

Barton, L. and Meighan, R. (1978) Sociological Interpretations of Schooling and Classrooms: a reappraisal. Driffield, Nafferton.

Barton L. and Tomlinson, S. (eds) (1984) *Special Education and Social Interests*. London, Croom Helm.

Barton, L. and Walker, R. (eds) (1978) *Sociological Interpretations of Schooling and Classrooms: a re-appraisal*. Driffield, Nafferton Books.

Bates, R.V. (1984) Educational versus Managerial Evaluation in Schools. In M.P. Broadfoot (ed.) *Selection, Certification and*

Control: Social Issues in Educational Assessment. Lewes, Falmer Press.

Bennett, N. (1985a) Interaction and Achievement in Classroom Groups. In N. Bennett and C. Desforges (eds) *Recent Advances in Classroom Research.* Edinburgh, Scottish Academic Press.

Bennett, N. (1985b) Time to Teach: Teaching-Learning Processes in Primary Schools. In N.J. Entwistle (ed.) *New Directions in Educational Psychology – Learning and Teaching.* Lewes, Falmer Press.

Bennett, N. and Blundell, D. (1983) Quantity and Quality of Work in Rows and Classroom Groups. *Educational Psychology*, 3, 93–105.

Bennett, N., Desforges, C., Cockburn, A. and Wilkinson, B. (1984) *The Quality of Pupil Learning Experiences.* London, Lawrence Erlbaum.

Berger, M. (1979) Behaviour Modification in Education and Professional Practice: The Dangers of a Mindless Technology. *Bulletin of the British Psychological Society*, 32, 418–19.

Berger, M. (1982) Applied Behaviour Analysis in Education: A Critical Assessment and Some Implications for Teachers. *Educational Psychology*, 2, 289–300.

Berliner, D.C. (1987) Ways of thinking about students and classrooms by more and less experienced teachers. In J. Calderhead (ed.) *Exploring Teachers' Thinking.* London, Cassell.

Beveridge, M. (ed.) (1982) *Children Thinking Through Language.* London, Edward Arnold.

Black, H.D. and Dockrell, W.B. (eds) (1988) *New Developments in Educational Assessment.* Edinburgh, Scottish Academic Press.

Bourdieu, P. (1977) Cultural Reproduction and Social Reproduction. In J. Karabel and A. H. Halsey (eds) *Power and Ideology in Education.* New York, Oxford University Press.

Bower, G.H. and Hildegard, E.R. (1981) *Theories of Learning.* Englewood Cliffs, NJ, Prentice-Hall.

Bowles, S. and Gintis, H. (1976) *Schooling in Capitalist America.* London, Routledge and Kegan Paul.

Boydell, D. (1975) Pupil Behaviour in Junior Classrooms. *British Journal of Educational Psychology*, 45, 122–9.

Brissenden, T. (1988) *Talking About Mathematics.* Oxford, Blackwell.

Broadfoot, P. (ed.) (1984) *Selection, Certification and Control: Social Issues in Educational Assessment.* Lewes, Falmer Press.

Broadfoot, P. (ed.) (1986) *Profiles and Records of Achievement: A Review of Issues and Practice.* Eastbourne, Holt, Rinehart and Winston.

Broadfoot, P. (1988) The National Assessment Framework and Records of Achievement. In H. Torrance (ed.) *National Assessment and Testing: A Research Response.* Kendal, British Educational Research Association.

Brown, M. (1989) Graded Assessment and Learning Hierarchies in Mathematics – An Alternative View. *British Educational Research Journal*, Vol. 15, No. 2, 121–8.

Brown, A. and De Loache, J. (1983) Metacognitive Skills. In M. Donaldson, R. Grieve and C. Pratt (eds) *Early Childhood Development and Education*. Oxford, Basil Blackwell.

Brown, G. and Desforges, C. (1979) *Piaget's Theory: a Psychological Critique*. London, Routledge and Kegan Paul.

Brown, G. A. and Edmondson, R. (1984) Asking Questions. In E. C. Wragg (ed.) *Classroom Teaching Skills*. London, Croom Helm.

Bruner, J. R. (1974) *Beyond The Information Given*. London, Allen and Unwin.

Bruner, J. R. (1986) *Actual Minds, Possible Worlds*. Cambridge, Mass., Harvard University Press.

Bruner, J. S. (1966) *Towards a Theory of Instruction,* Cambridge, Mass: CUP.

CACE (Central Advisory Council on Education) (1967) *Children and Their Primary Schools* (The Plowden Report). London, HMSO.

Callaghan, J. (1976) *Speech by the Prime Minister*, the Rt. Hon. James Callaghan MP, at a foundation stone-laying ceremony at Ruskin College, Oxford, on Monday, 18 October (press release).

Carlberg, C. and Kavale, K. (1980) Efficacy of Special versus Regular Class Placement for Exceptional Children: a meta-analysis. *Journal of Special Education*, 14, 295–309.

Carter, K. and Doyle, W. (1987) Teachers' Knowledge Structures and Comprehension Processes. In J. Calderhead (ed.) *Exploring Teachers' Thinking*. London, Cassell.

Chapman, P. D. (1981) Schools as Sorters: testing and tracking in California, 1910–1925. *Journal of Social History*, 14, 701–17.

Chi, M.T.H. (1978) Knowledge structures and memory development. In R. S. Seiger (ed.) *Children's Thinking: What Develops?* Hillsdale, Lawrence Erlbaum.

Chi, M.T.H. (1981) Knowledge Development and Memory Performance. In M.P. Friedman, J.P. Das and N. O'Connor (eds) *Intelligence and Learning*. New York, Plenum Press.

Claxton, G., Swann, W., Salmon, P., Walkerdine, V., Jacobsen, B. and White, J. (1985) *Psychology and Schooling: What's the Matter?* Bedford Way Papers, 25. London, University of London Institute of Education.

Cohen, L. and Manion, L. (1981) *Perspectives on Schools and Classrooms*. London, Holt, Rinehart and Winston.

Cole, M. (1985) The Zone of Proximal Development: where culture and cognition create each other. In J.V. Wertsch (ed.) *Culture Communication and Cognition*. Cambridge, Cambridge University Press.

Coleman, J. S. *et al.* (1966) Equality of Educational Opportunity, Washington, US Government Printing Office.

Craik, F.I.M. and Tulving, E. (1975) Depth of processing and the retention of words in episodic memory. *Journal of Experimental Psychology*, 104, 268–94.

Croll, P. and Moses, D. (1988) Teaching Methods and Time on Task in Junior Classrooms. *Educational Research*, 30, 90–7.

David, K. and Charlton, T. (eds) (1987) *The Caring Role of the Primary School*. London, Macmillan.

Davie, R., Butler, N. and Goldstein, H. (1972) *From Birth to Seven*. London, Longman.

Department of Education and Science (1975) *The Discovery of Children Requiring Special Education and the Assessment of their Needs*. (Circular 2/75). London, DES.

Department of Education and Science (DES) (1978a) *Special Educational Needs* (The Warnock Report). London, HMSO.

Department of Education and Science (DES) (1978b) *Primary Education in England*. London, HMSO.

Department of Education and Science (DES) (1981) *West Indian Children in Our Schools. Interim Report of the Committee of Inquiry into the Education of Children from Ethnic Minority Groups*. Chairman Anthony Rampton. London, HMSO.

Department of Education and Science (DES) (1982) *Mathematics Counts: Report of the Committee of Inquiry into the Teaching of Mathematics in Schools*. Chairman W.H. Cockcroft. London, HMSO.

Department of Education and Science (DES) (1985) *Better Schools*. London, HMSO.

Department of Education and Science (DES) (1988a) *School Teachers' Pay and Conditions of Service Document*. London, DES.

Department of Education and Science (DES) (1988b) *LEA Training Grants Scheme: Training to Meet the Special Educational Needs of Pupils with Learning Difficulties in Schools: Guidance Note* (Teacher Training Circular Letter 1/88). London, DES.

Department of Education and Science (DES) (1988c) *Report of the Committee of Inquiry into the teaching of English language*. Chairman Sir John Kingman. London, HMSO.

Department of Education and Science (DES) (1988d) *National Curriculum Task Group on Assessment and Testing. A Report*. London, DES.

Department of Education and Science (DES) (1989a) *Initial Teacher Training: Approval of Courses* (Circular 24/89). London, DES.

Department of Education and Science (DES) (1989b) *Education Reform Act 1988: Temporary Exceptions from the National Curriculum*. London, DES.

Department of Education and Science (DES) (1989c) *National Curriculum: From Policy to Practice*. London, DES.

Department of Education and Science and Her Majesty's Inspectors of Schools (DES, HMI) (1977) *Curriculum 11–16*. London, DES.

Diener, C.I. and Dweck, C. (1978) An Analysis of Learned Helplessness: Continuous Changes on Performance, Strategy, and Achievement Cognitions Following Failure. *Journal of Personality and Social Psychology*, 36, 451–62.

Donaldson, M. (1978) *Children's Minds*. London, Fontana.

Doyle, W. (1983) Academic Work. *Review of Educational Research*, 53, 159–99.

Doyle, W. (1986) Classroom Organisation and Management. In M.C. Wittrock (ed.) *Handbook of Research on Teaching*, 3rd edn. New York, Macmillan.

Doyle, W. and Carter, K. (1984) Academic Tasks in Classrooms. *Curriculum Inquiury*, 14, 129–49.

Driver, R. (1983) *The Pupil as Scientist*. Milton Keynes, Open University Press.

Dugdale, R.L. (1977) *The Jukes: A Study on Crime, Pauperism, Disease and Heredity*. 5th Edition, New York, G. T. Putnam.

Duncan, A. and Dunn, W. (1988) *What Primary Teachers Should Know About Assessment*. London, Hodder and Stoughton.

Dunham, J. (1984) *Stress in Teaching*. London, Croom Helm.

Durkheim, E. (1952) *Suicide*. London, Routledge and Kegan Paul.

Dweck, C., Davidson, W., Nelson, S. and Enna, B. (1978) Sex Differences in Learned Helplessness: the contingencies of evaluative feedback in the classroom and an experimental analysis. *Developmental Psychology*, 14, 268–76.

Dweck, C. and Wortman, C. B. (1982) Learned Helplessness, Anxiety and Achievement Motivation. In H.W. Krohne and L. Laux (eds) *Achievement, Stress and Anxiety*. London, Hemisphere.

Edelwick, J. and Brodsky, A. (1980) *Burn-out: Stages of Disillusionment in the Helping Professions*. New York, Human Sciences Press.

Edwards, A. (1984) *The Development of Self in the Pre-school Child*. Unpublished PhD Thesis, University of Wales.

Edwards, A. (1988) A Child of Four Could Tell You. In F. Fransella and L. Thomas (eds) *Experimenting With Personal Construct Psychology*. London, Routledge and Kegan Paul.

Eisner, E.W. (1985) *The Educational Imagination: On the Design and Evaluation of School Programs*. London, Macmillan.

Evans, R. and Ferguson, N. (1974) Screening School Entrants. *Association of Educational Psychologists Journal*, 3, 2–9.

Fisher, C.W., Filby, N.N., Marliave, R., Cahe, L.S., Dishaw, M.M., Moore, J.E. and Berliner, D.C. (1978) *Teaching Behaviours, Academic Learning Time and Student Achievement.* San Francisco, BTES: Far West Laboratory.

Floyd, A. (1981) *Developing Mathematical Thinking.* London, Addison Wesley for the Open University Press.

Fogelman, K. (1976) *Britain's Sixteen Year Olds.* London, National Children's Bureau.

Fontana, D. (1984) Failures of Academic Achievement. In A. Gale and A.J. Chapman (eds), *Psychology and Social Problems.* London, Macmillan/BPS.

French, J. and French, P. (1984) Gender Imbalances in the Primary Classroom: An Interactionist Account. *Educational Research,* 26, 127–36.

French, J.P. and Peskett, R. (1986) Control instructions in the infant classroom *Educational Research,* 28, 210–19.

Galloway, D. (1985) *Schools and Persistent Absentees.* Oxford: Pergamon.

Galloway, D. (1987) Teachers, Parents and Other Professionals. In K. David and T. Charlton (eds) *The Caring Role of the Primary School.* London, Macmillan.

Galloway, D. (1990) Was the GERBIL a Marxist Mole? In P. Evans and V. Varma (eds) *Special Education, Past, Present and Future.* London, Falmer Press.

Galloway, D., Boswell, K., Panckhurst, F., Boswell, C. and Green, K. (1985) Sources of Satisfaction and Dissatisfaction for New Zealand Primary School Teachers. *Educational Research,* 27, 44–51.

Galloway, D. and Goodwin, C. (1987) *The Education of Disturbing Children: pupils with learning and adjustment difficulties.* London, Longman.

Galloway, D., Panckhurst, F., Buswell, K., Boswell, C. and Green, K. (1986) Sources of Stress for Primary School Head Teachers in New Zealand. *British Educational Research Journal,* 12, 281–8.

Galloway, D. and Rogers, C. (1990) Disruptive Behaviour, Effective Schooling and Motivational Style. In P. Maher (ed.) *Juvenile Crime: The Educational Perspective.* Oxford, Basil Blackwell (forthcoming).

Galton, M., Simon, B. and Croll, P. (1980) *Inside the Primary Classroom.* London, Routledge and Kegan Paul.

Galton, M. and Simon, B. (eds) (1980) *Progress and Performance in the Primary Classroom.* London, Routledge and Kegan Paul.

Galton, M. and Willcocks, J. (eds) (1983) *Moving from the Primary Classroom.* London, Routledge and Kegan Paul.

Gipps, C., Cross, H. and Goldstein, H. (1987) Warrock's Eighteen Per Cent: Children with special needs in Primary Schools. Lewes, Falmer Press.

Goacher, B., Evans, J., Welton, J. and Wedell, K. (1988) *Policy and Provision for Special Educational Needs: Implementing the 1981 Education Act*. London, Cassell.

Goldstein, H. (1987) *Multilevel Models in Educational and Social Research*. New York, Oxford University Press.

Goldstein, H. (1988) Comparing Schools in H. Torrance (ed.) *National Assessment and Testing: A Research Response*. Kendal, British Educational Research Association.

Gruendel, J.M. (1977) Referential Extension in Early Language Development. *Child Development*, 48, 1567–76.

Habermas, J. (1972) *Knowledge and Human Interests*. London, Heinemann.

Hargreaves, A. (1986) Ideological Recordbreakers. In P. Broadfoot (ed). *Profiles and Records of Achievement*. Eastbourne, Holt Educational.

Hargreaves, A. (1988) *Personal and Social Education: Choices and Challenges*. Oxford, Basil Blackwell.

Hargreaves, D. (1982) *Challenge for the Comprehensive School: Culture, Curriculum, Community*. London, Routledge and Kegan Paul.

Harlen, W. (1989) The National Curriculum in Science in *Primary Education and the National Curriculum*. Association for the Study of Primary Education.

Harlen, W., Darwin, A., and Murphy, M.C. (1977) *Match and Mismatch: Raising Questions*. Edinburgh, Oliver and Boyd.

Harré, R. (1979) *Social Being*. Oxford, Basil Blackwell.

Harré, R. (1983) *Personal Being*. Oxford, Basil Blackwell.

Harrop, A. (1983) *Behaviour Modification in the Classroom*. London, Hodder and Stoughton.

Haviland, D. (1988) *Take Care, Mr. Baker!*, London, Fourth Estate.

Heal, K.H. (1978) Misbehaviour Among School Children: The Role of the School in Strategies for Prevention. *Policy and Politics*, 6, 321–32.

Hearnshaw, L.S. (1979) *Cyril Burt: Psychologist*. London, Hodder and Stoughton.

Hegarty, S. (1987) *Meeting Special Needs in Ordinary Schools*. London, Cassell.

Hewison, J. and Tizard, J. (1980) Parental Involvement and Reading Attainment. *British Journal of Education Psychology*, 50, 209–15.

Hindley, C.B. and Owen, C.F. (1978) The Extent of Individual Changes in IQ for Ages Between 6 months and 17 years in a British Longitudinal Sample. *Journal of Child Psychology and Psychiatry*, 19, 329–50.

Hockaday, F. (1984) Collaborative Learning with Young Children. *Educational Studies*, 10, 237–42.

Holdaway, E.A. (1978) Facet and Overall Satisfaction of Teachers. *Education Administration Quarterly*, 14, 30–47.

Holt, M. (1987) Bureaucratic Benefits. *Times Educational Supplement*, 18 September, 30.

Horton, T. and Raggatt, P. (eds) (1982) *Challenge and Change in the Curriculum*. London, Hodder and Stoughton.

House of Commons (1987) Education, Science and Arts Committee, *3: Report: Special Educational Needs: Implementation of the 1987 Act*, HMSO.

Humphries, S. (1981) *Hooligans or Rebels? An Oral History of Working Class Childhood and Youth, 1889–1939*. Oxford, Basil Blackwell.

Inner London Education Authority (ILEA) (1985) *Equal Opportunities for All?* (The Fish Report). London, ILEA.

Inner London Education Authority (ILEA) (1988) *The Primary Language Record: Handbook for Teachers*. London, Centre for Language in Primary Education, ILEA.

Johnson, D. and Ransom, E. (1983) *Family and School*. London, Croom Helm.

Joseph, K. (1983) *Address to Council of Local Education Authorities*. 16 July. Unpublished.

Kamin, L.J. (1974) *The Science and Politics of IQ*. New York, Erlbaum.

Kelly, G. (1955) *A Theory of Personality*. New York, Norton.

Knight, P. and Smith, L. (1989) In Search of Good Practice. *Journal of Curriculum Practice*, 21, 427–40.

Kohlberg, L. (1975) The Cognitive Developmental Approach to Moral Education. *Phi Delta Kappa*, 56, 670–7.

Kolvin, I., Garside, R.D., Nicol, A.R., Macmillan, A., Wolstenholme, F. and Leitsch, I.M. (1981) *Help Starts Here: The Maladjusted Child in the Ordinary School*. London, Tavistock.

Lang, P. (ed.) (1988) *Thinking About Personal and Social Education in the Primary School*. Oxford, Basil Blackwell.

Law, B. (1984) *Uses and Abuses of Profiling*. London, Harper and Row.

Levitt, E. E. (1963) Results of Psychotherapy with Children: a further evaluation. *Behaviour, Research and Therapy*, 1, 45–51.

Lynas, W. (1985) *Integrating the Handicapped into Ordinary Schools: A Study of Hearing Impaired Pupils*. London, Croom Helm.

McClure, S. (1989) *Education Reformed*. London, Hodder & Stoughton.

McNamara, D. (1988) Objectives or Aspirations? *Review* (of the Education Section of the British Psychological Society), 12, ii, 39–47.

Macbeth, A (1984) *The Child Between: A Report on School-Family Relations in Countries of the EEC*. European Community, HMSO.

Marland, M. (1985) Parents, Schooling and the Welfare of Pupils. In P. Ribbins (ed.) *Schooling and Welfare.* Lewes, Falmer Press.

Maslow, A.H. (1970) *Motivation and Personality* (2nd edn.). New York, Harper and Row.

Mead, G.H. (1934) *Mind, Self and Society.* Chicago, Chicago University Press.

Merrett, F. and Wheldall, K. (1986) Observing Pupils and Teachers in Classrooms (OPTIC): A Behavioural Observation Schedule for Use in Schools. *Educational Psychology,* 6, 57–70.

Metge, J. and Kinloch, P. (1978) *Talking Past Each Other: Problems of Cross Cultural Communications.* Wellington, New Zealand. Victoria, University of Wellington.

Middleton, D. and Edwards, D. (eds) (1990) *Collective Remembering.* London, Sage.

Moon, C. (1984) Making Use of Miscues When Children Read Aloud, in: *Children Reading to Their Teachers.* National Association for the Teaching of English.

Mortimore, J. and Blackstone, T. (1982) *Disadvantage and Education.* London, Heinemann.

Mortimore, P., Sammons, P., Stoll, G., Lewis, D. and Ecob, R. (1988) *School Matters: The Junior Years.* Wells, Open Books.

Moyle, D. (1979) Informal Testing and Reading Needs in M. Raggett, C. Tutt, and P. Raggett (eds) *Assessment and Testing of Reading: Problems and Practices.* London, Ward Lock Educational.

Nash, R. (1983) Four Charges against TOSCA. *New Zealand Journal of Educational Studies,* 18, 154–65.

National Curriculum Council (1989) *Interim Report to the Secretary of State on Cross-Curricular Issues.* York, NCC.

Nelson, K. (1977) The Conceptual Basis of Naming. In J. MacNamara (ed.) *Language Learning and Thought.* New York, Academic Press.

Newson, J. (1974) Towards a theory of infant understanding. *Bulletin of the British Psychological Society.* 27, 251–7.

Newson, J. (1977) An Intersubjective Approach to the Systematic Description of Mother-Infant Interaction. In H.R. Schaffer (ed.) *Studies in Mother-Infant Interaction.* London, Academic Press.

Nicholls, J. (1984) *Advances in Motivation and Achievement: Vol 3 The Development of Achievement Motivation.* London, JAI Press.

Nisbet, J. and Shucksmith, J. (1986) *Learning Strategies.* London, Routledge and Kegan Paul.

Norman, D.A. (1978) Notes towards a complex theory of learning. In A.M. Lesgold, J. W. Pellegrino, S. D. Fokkema and R. Glaser (eds) *Cognitive Psychology and Instruction.* New York, Plenum.

Noss, R., Goldstein, H., Hoyles, C. (1989) Graded Assessment and Learning Hierarchies in Mathematics. *British Educational Research Journal,* 15, 109–20.

Nuttall, D. (1981) *School Self-Evaluation: Accountability with a Human Face*. London, Schools Council.

O'Leary, K.D. and O'Lear, S.C. (1979) *Classroom Management: The Successful Use of Behaviour Modification in the Classroom*. New York, Pergamon.

Pearson, L. and Lindsay, G. (1986) *Special Needs in the Primary School*. Windsor, NFER-Nelson.

Pervin, L. (1984) Am I me or am I the situation? in P. Barnes, J. Oates, J. Chapman, V. Lee and P. Czerniewska (eds), *Personality, Development and Learning*, Sevenoaks, Hodder and Stoughton.

Piaget, J. (1936) *The Origin of Intelligence in the Child* (trans. M. Cook, 1977) Harmondsworth, Penguin.

Pollard, A. and Tann, S. (1987) *Reflective Teaching in the Primary School*. London, Cassell.

Pratt, J. (1985) The Attitudes of Teachers. In J. Whyte, R. Deem, L. Kant and M. Cruikshank (eds) *Girl-Friendly Schooling*. London, Methuen.

Preston, R.C. (1962) Reading Achievement of German and American Children. *School and Society*, 90, 350–4.

Pring, R.A. (1984) *Personal and Social Education in the Curriculum*. London, Hodder and Stoughton.

Pritchard, K. and Richmond, K. (1989) *The Records of Achievement Manual*. New York, Longman.

Pumfrey, P. (1979) Which Test? In M. Raggett, C. Tutt and P. Raggett (eds) *Assessment and Testing of Reading: Problems and Practices*. London, Ward Lock Educational.

Purkey, S.C. and Smith, M.S. (1983) Effective Schools: a review. *Elementary School Journal*, 83, 427–52.

Ramasut, A. (ed.) (1989) *Whole School Approaches to Special Needs*. Lewes, Falmer Press.

Reynolds, D. (ed.) (1985) *Studying School Effectiveness*. Lewes, Falmer Press.

Richards, M. and Light, P. (eds) (1986) *Children of Social Worlds*. Cambridge, Polity Press.

Roberts, T. (1979) The Hidden Curriculum in the Infants School. *Durham and Newcastle Research Review*, 8, 42, 29–33.

Rubinstein, D. (1969) *School Attendance in London, 1870–1904: A Social History*. Hull, University of Hull.

Rutter, M. (1966) *Children of Sick Parents: An Environmental and Psychiatric Study*. Institute of Psychiatric Study. Institute of Psychiatry, Mandsley Monographs No 16. London, Oxford University Press.

Rutter, M. (1981) Stress, Coping and Development: some issues and some questions. *Journal of Child Psychology and Psychiatry*, 22, 323–56.

Rutter, M., Cox, A., Tupling, C., Berger, M. and Yule, W. (1975) Attainment and Adjustment in two Geographical Areas: 1. The Prevalence of Psychiatric Disorder. *British Journal of Psychiatry*, 126, 493–509.

Rutter, M. and Madge, N. (1976) *Cycles of Disadvantage*. London, Heinemann.

Rutter, M., Maughan, B., Mortimore, P. and Ouston, T. (1979) *Fifteen Thousand Hours: Secondary Schools and their Effects on Pupils*. London, Open Books.

Rutter, M., Tizard, J. and Whitmore, K. (1970) *Education, Health and Behaviour*. London, Longman.

Salmon, P. and Claire, H. (1984) *Classroom Collaboration*. London, Routledge and Kegan Paul.

Sampson, O.C. (1975) *Remedial Education*. London, Routledge and Kegan Paul.

Saxe, G., Guberman, S. and Gearhart, M. (1987) Social Processes in Early Number Development. *Monographs of the Society for Research in Child Development*, Serial No. 216, 52, 2.

Schaffer, H.R. (1977) *Mothering*. London, Fontana.

Scottish Education Department (1978) *The Education of Pupils with Learning Difficulties in Primary and Secondary Schools: A Progress Report by Her Majesty's Inspectorate*. Edinburgh, HMSO.

Sharp, R. and Green, A.G. (1975) *Education and Social Control*. London, Routledge and Kegan Paul.

Shayer, M. and Adey, P. (1981) *Towards a Science of Science Teaching*. London, Heinemann.

Shipman, M. (1983) *Assessment in Primary and Middle Schools*. London, Croom Helm.

Shotter, J. (1984) *Social Accountability and Selfhood*. Oxford, Basil Blackwell.

Simmons, K. (1986) Painful Extractions. *Times Educational Supplement*, 17 October.

Simon, B.(1989) *The Great Schooling Scandal*. London, Lawrence and Wishart.

Simons, H. (1987) *Getting to Know Schools in a Democracy*. Lewes, Falmer Press.

Skilbeck, M. (ed.) (1984) *Evaluating the Curriculum in the Eighties*. London, Hodder and Stoughton.

Smith, D.J. and Tomlinson, S. (1989) *The School Effect: A study of multi-racial comprehensives*. London, Policy Studies Institute.

Stenhouse, L. (1975) *An Introduction to Curriculum Research and Development*. London, Heinemann Educational.

Stone, M. (1981) *The Education of the Black Child in Britain*. London, Fontana.

Sutherland, M. (1988) *Theory of Education*. London, Longman.

Sutton, A. (1983) An Introduction to Soviet Psychology. In S. Meadows (ed.) *Developing Thinking*. London, Methuen.

Swann, W. (1985) Is the Integration of Children with Special Needs Happening? An Analysis of Recent Statistics for Pupils in Special Schools. *Oxford Review of Education*, 11, 3–18.

Tajfel, H. (1978) Intergroup Behaviour: II Group Perspectives. In H. Tajfel and C. Fraser (eds) *Introducing Social Psychology*. London, Penguin.

Tann, C.S. (1981) Grouping and Group Work. In B. Simon and J. Willcocks (eds) *Research and Practice in the Primary Classroom*. London, Routledge and Kegan Paul.

Taylor, C. (1977) What is Human Agency? In T. Mischel (ed.) *The Self: Psychological and Philosophical Issues*. Oxford, Basil Blackwell.

Tizard, B., Blatchford, P., Berke, J., Farquhar, C., and Plewis, I. (1988) *Young Children at School in the Inner City*. Hove, Erlbaum.

Tizard, B. and Hughes, M. (1984) *Young Children Learning*. London, Fontana.

Tizard, J., Schofield, W.N. and Hewison, J. (1982) Collaboration between Teachers and Parents in Assisting Children's Reading. *British Journal of Educational Psychology*, 52, 1–15.

Tobin, D. and Pumfrey, P. (1976) Some Long-term Effects of the Remedial Teaching of Reading. *Educational Review*, 29, 1–12.

Tomlinson, S. (1980) The educational performance of ethnic minority children, *New Community*, 8, 213–234.

Tomlinson, S. (1982) *The Ecology of Special Education*. London, Routledge and Kegan Paul.

Tomlinson, S. (1984) *Home and School in Multicultural Britain*. London, Batsford.

Torrance, H. (ed.) (1988) *National Assessment and Testing: A Research Response*. British Educational Research Association.

Training Agency (1990) *Youth Cohort study: Education and Training Opportunities in the Inner City*. Bradford, Training Agency.

Trevarthen, C. (1974) Conversations with a one month old. *New Scientist*, 62, 230–35.

Trevarthen, C. (1977) Descriptive Analyses of Infant Communicative Behaviour. In H.R. Schaffer (ed.) *Studies in Mother–Infant Interaction*. London, Academic Press.

Trevarthen, C. (1979) Instincts for human understanding and for cultural cooperation: their development in infancy. In M. Von Cranach, K. Foppa, W. Le Peines and D. Ploog (eds) *Human Ethology*. Cambridge, Cambridge University Press.

Tutt, N. (1985) The Unintended Consequences of Integration. *Educational and Child Psychology*, 2, iii, 30–8.

Tyler, S. (1980) *Keele Pre-school Assessment Guide*. Windsor, NFER-Nelson.

Vincent, D., Green, L., Francis, J. and Powney, J. (1983) *A Review of Reading Tests*. Windsor, NFER-Nelson.

Vogelaar, L. M. E. and Silverman, M. S. (1984) Non-verbal Communication in Cross-cultural Counselling: A literature view. *International Journal for the Advancement of Counselling*, 7, 41–57.

Vygotsky, L.S. (1962) *Thought and Language*. New York, Wiley.

Vygotsky, L.S. (1978) *Mind in Society*, M. Cole, V. John-Steiner, S. Scribner and E. Souberman (eds) Cambridge, Mass., Harvard University Press.

Walden, R. and Walkerdine, V. (1985) *Girls and Mathematics: From Primary to Secondary Schooling*. Bedford Way Paper No 24. London, Institute of Education, University of London.

Walkerdine, V. (1984) Developmental Psychology and the Child-Centred Pedagogy: the insertion of Piaget in early education. M. J. Henriques, W. Hollway, C. Urwin, C. Venn and V. Walkerdine (eds) *Changing the subject*. London, Methuen.

Walkerdine, V. and Sinha, C. (1978) The Internal Triangle: language, reasoning and the social context. In I. Markova (ed.) *The Social Context of Language*. Chichester, Wiley.

Wedge, P. and Essen, J. (1982) *Children in Adversity*. London, Pan.

Wedge, P. and Prosser, U. (1973) *Born to Fail?* London, Arrow Books.

Weiner, B. (1979) *A Theory of Motivation for some Classroom Experiences. Journal of Educational Psychology*, 71, 3–25.

Weiner, B. (1984) Principles for a Theory of Student Motivation and their Application within an Attributionist Framework. In Ames, R. E. and Ames, C. (eds) *Research on Motivation in Education, Vol I: Student Motivation*. London, Academic Press.

Wells, G. (1981) Becoming a Communicator. In G. Wells (ed.) *Learning Through Interaction*. Cambridge, Cambridge University Press.

Wertsch, J.L. (ed.) (1984) *Culture, Communication and Cognition*: Vygotskian Perspectives. Cambridge, Cambridge University Press.

West, C. and Wheldall, K. (1989) Waiting for Teacher: the frequency and duration of times children spend waiting for teacher attention in infant school classrooms. *British Educational Research Journal*, 15, 205–16.

Wheldall, K. (1982) Behavioural Pedagogy or Behavioural Overkill. *Educational Psychology*, 2, 181–4.

Wheldall, K. (1985) The Use of Behavioural Ecology in Classroom Management. In N. Entwistle (ed.) *New Directions in Educational Psychology*. Vol. 1, Learning and Teaching. Lewes, Falmer Press.

Wheldall, K. and Glynn, T. (1989) *Effective Classroom Learning*. Oxford, Basil Blackwell.

Wheldall, K. and Merrett, F. (1984) *Positive Teaching: The Behavioural Approach*. London, Allen and Unwin.

Wheldall, K. and Merrett, F. (1985) The Behavioural Approach to Teaching Package (BATPACK): an experimental evaluation. *British Journal of Educational Psychology*, 55, 65–75.

Wheldall, K., Morris, M., Vaughan, P. and Yin Yuk Ng (1981) Rows v Tables: An example of the Use of Behavioural Ecology in Two Classes of Eleven Year Old Children. *Educational Psychology*, 1, 171–83.

White, J. (1988) *The Language of Science*. A report prepared for the Assessment of Performance Unit. London, DES.

White, R.W. (1959) Motivation Reconsidered: the concept of competence. *Psychological Review*, 66, 297–333.

Whitty, G. and Young, M. (eds) (1976) *Explorations in the Politics of School Knowledge*. Driffield, Nafferton.

Whyte, J. (1983) *Beyond the Wendy House: sex role stereotyping in primary schools*. York, Longman.

Widlake, P. and Macleod, F. (1984) *Raising Standards: Parental Involvement Programmes and the Language Performance of Children*. Coventry, Community Education Development Centre.

Willes, M. (1981) Children Becoming Pupils. In C. Adelman (ed.) *Uttering Muttering*. London, Grant McIntyre.

Willis, P. (1977) *Learning to Labour: How Working Class Kids get Working Class Jobs*. London, Saxon House.

Wood, D, (1988) *How Children Think and Learn*. Oxford, Basil Blackwell.

Woods, P. (ed.) (1980a) *Teacher Strategies*. London, Croom Helm.

Woods, P. (ed.) (1980b) *Pupil Strategies*. London, Croom Helm.

Woods, P. and Hammersley, M. (eds) (1977) *School Experience*. London, Croom Helm.

Woolfolk, A.E. and Nicholich, L. M. (1980) *Educational Psychology for Teachers*. Englewood Cliffs, NJ, Prentice-Hall.

Yeomans, A. (1983) Collaborative Group Work in Primary and Secondary Schools: Britain and the USA. *Durham and Newcastle Research Review*, 10, 51, 99–105.

Young, P. and Tyre, C. (1983) *Dyslexia or Illiteracy? Realising the Right to Read*. Milton Keynes, Open University Press.

Zeichner, K.M., Tabachnick, B.R. and Densmore, K. (1987) Individual, Institutional and Cultural Influences on the Development of Teachers' Craft Knowledge. In J. Calderhead (ed.) *Exploring Teachers' Thinking*. London, Cassell.